OXFORD PAPERBACKS
HANDBOOKS FOR ARTISTS
General Editors: Quentin Bell and Lynton Lamb

10. Silk-screen Printing

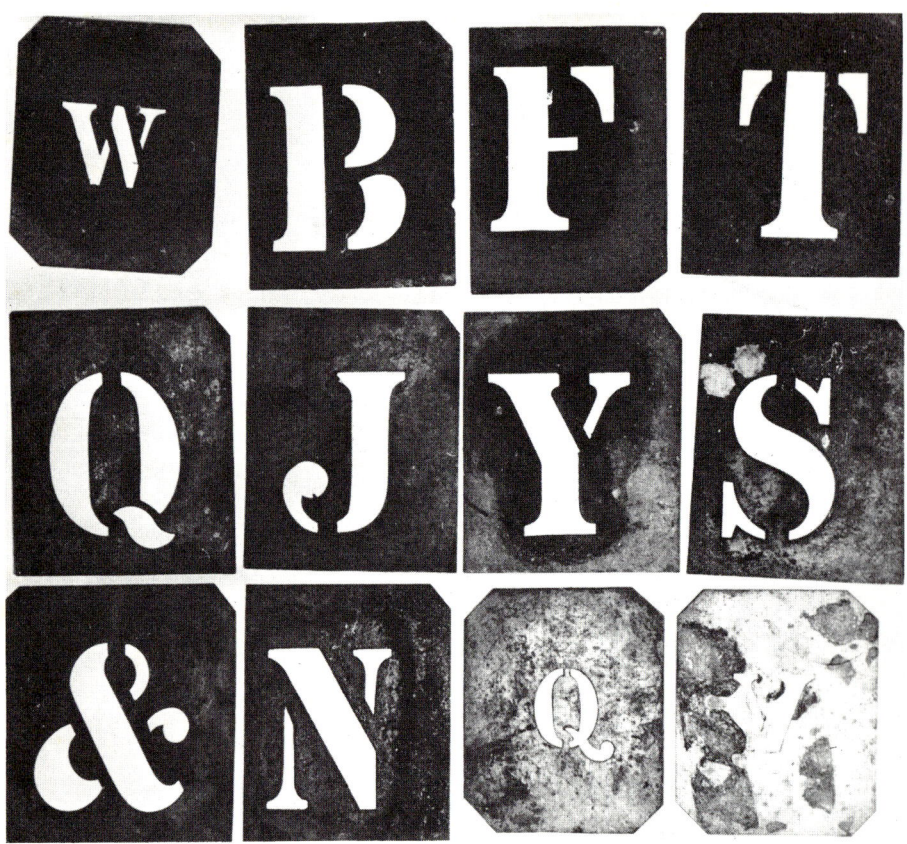

Fig. 1
Packing-case letters

Silk-screen Printing

BRIAN ELLIOTT

LONDON
Oxford University Press
NEW YORK · TORONTO
1971

Oxford University Press, Ely House, London W.1

GLASGOW   NEW YORK   TORONTO   MELBOURNE   WELLINGTON
CAPE TOWN   SALISBURY   IBADAN   NAIROBI   DAR ES SALAAM   LUSAKA   ADDIS ABABA
BOMBAY   CALCUTTA   MADRAS   KARACHI   LAHORE   DACCA
KUALA LUMPUR   SINGAPORE   HONG KONG   TOKYO

ISBN 19 289914 7
© *Oxford University Press* 1971

Screen prints and diagrams are the author's.
Photographs of processes taken by Denis Masi.

Set by Keyspools Ltd, Golborne, Lancs.
and printed in Great Britain
at the University Press, Oxford
by Vivian Ridler
Printer to the University

Contents

   Introduction 6
1. Historical 7
2. The Screen and other Equipment 12
3. Ink and Paper 23
4. The Stencil I 30
5. The Stencil II 47
6. Transfer Printing, Vacuum Forming, and Mould Blowing 58
7. Photography 65
8. Photo Silk-screen 75
   List of Suppliers 84
   Index 85

Introduction

In writing a book about technique such as this I have avoided diagrams of ideal studios, dream palaces for graphic artists, and so on. The conditions that most of you will be working under are more like those of an early Beckett play than the creation of some ergonomic genius. I have also tried to keep mystification to a minimum: if there is to be any mystery it should have no place in the technique. A beautiful process is too often completely spoilt by people who surround it with an elaborate jargon that becomes a mere badge of 'in-ness'. A technique is to be used: it should not get in the way of creation; it should be an unobtrusive part of it.

I have also tried to give some indication of the margins of error. These are wider than most manufacturers are prepared to admit. In this respect I am aware that with certain procedures (and particularly with photography) I have been perhaps unnecessarily cautious because I feel that it is ridiculous to treat a mere indication of method as a hard and fast rule. The techniques I have described will be carried out in conditions as varied as the prints they will produce. The only rules are those that the artist himself discovers: therefore, I have not tried to give rules so much as to indicate possible directions. For me the ideal would be one long accident or at least the recognition that such is the natural condition of life.

CHAPTER 1

Historical

The silk-screen printing process in its present-day form is not very old: just a little more than fifty years. But as silk-screen is a direct development from, and is itself a stencil process, we must therefore, in examining its history, deal in part with the far more ancient history of stencils. Examples of stencils can be found in China dating back to at least the construction of the Great Wall and in Egypt to the time of the pyramids. The application of the process was decorative, used on pottery, fabrics, and buildings. It acquired a mystic significance with the Buddhists and there are examples of the image of Buddha made with stencils. The early results are generally crude, as befits the materials used, yet the basic idea had been established: holes cut or punched into sheets of papyrus, skins, or fabrics. These were made impervious to the pigments to be used by lacquer (shcllac) or animal fats, which also lengthened the life of the stencil. The stencils were placed upon the surface to be printed and the pigment was brushed through the holes as it is today with packing-case letters.

The initial development was not to be seriously superseded for many years. The results must have been regarded as roughly satisfactory. Wood blocks were eventually used if any finer details were needed. Stencils were relegated to the coarser jobs needing heavier layers of pigment and where delicacy was not required. Strangely, the resulting prejudice survives to this day. In Japan, however, the development of stencils was pushed much further as the demand grew for decorating fabrics. The delicacy now required meant that finely cut stencils would need strengthening if they were not to break; and raw silk thread was introduced as a support. The method was still extremely simple, two sheets of paper were cut at the same time and then taken apart. The silk thread was laid on one sheet and pasted into position, the complementary sheet was placed on top making a sandwich. Finally the whole would be lacquered to strengthen it and make it impervious. It was now possible to cut stencils of extreme delicacy.

But there was a further significant achievement involved: the silk thread made it possible to have 'islands'. For example, the most distinctive features of the packing-case alphabet are the bridges which hold the centres of the letters. If these were, instead of bands of metal, fine threads of silk, then the ink would be uninterrupted and thus the bridge would not appear in the print. This the Japanese soon realized and were quick to exploit with images of the greatest delicacy and complexity. Obviously sooner or later someone was going to tire of tying or pasting hundreds of threads to a stencil and would simply stick the stencil to a woven piece of silk. There remained one more step: to stretch the silk to a wooden frame. Having done this they had invented silk-screen printing. There is no information as to whether any individual was responsible for this invention. I greatly doubt it; it is more likely to be the collective effort of generations in the face of a growing demand for finer fabric designs.

The factors involved in the development of the screen process in the West are somewhat confused, yet they are none the less interesting. The major question seems to be why was it left to the U.S.A. to develop it into a technique—the application of which is quite literally as vast as it is varied. For it became known initially in Europe, with the great discovery of Japanese culture in the late nineteenth century. Maybe it was simply seen as a stencil technique. This, combined with enormous preoccupation with industry and its complex machines and all the 'romance' therein, would probably have been enough to force it for Europeans into the quaint oriental, non-scientific, non-technological, clever class—in other words a craft, unworthy of Victorian technocrats. However, there were a few people interested in it and patents were taken out; but this did not aid its development or its acceptance. It only served to stifle it.

If we now look across the Atlantic we see that the situation was quite different. In the early nineteenth century a population of immigrants from a variety of countries, brought their various trades, crafts, and skills to a land where the machine was still a novelty and mass-produced articles were imported from Europe. These articles were decorated individually by means of stencils, and are now prized items for the collector. We have there a situation ripe for the development of the screen process since there was a general lack of suitable machinery in America, the Europeans being too busy exporting printed fabrics to export as well the machines to print the fabric with. Early in this century many patents were taken out on a variety of techniques still used in America. The English can claim only one major early breakthrough worthy of note. It is the invention around 1929 of basic photo-screen process. The twenties also saw the first machine for printing with screens, speeds of up to 1,500 impressions an hour (i.p.h.) being achieved. There are now machines that go beyond 3,000 i.p.h; and really silk-screen is no more limited by speed than any other process. The invention of such machines brought the process onto a level commercially competitive with other techniques: and here we see its final acceptance. There is still a lot of prejudice against the process, particularly for fine art work; and strangely enough, at the time of writing, this prejudice is strongest in the country that did most for its general acceptance and commercial exploitation, that is, the U.S.A. But then they also find it difficult to accept autographic off-set lithography.

To give a complete picture of the history of screen process printing, it is necessary to refer to some other related techniques. *Pochoir* is a method which is now little used as a means of reproduction. However at one time it was considered (and still is by many people) as the best printing process for reproduction purposes ever used. The only country that still uses it to my knowledge is Switzerland. Strictly speaking it belongs to the age of the hand-coloured lithograph. It consists of cutting a series of stencils, one for each colour of the picture to be reproduced, a form of colour separation dependent solely on the human eye. The more expensive the reproduction the greater the amount of stencils cut, the finer the chromatic breakdown. When completed, the colour is applied by hand and can be carried within the particular printing area to obtain even greater subtleties. With the perfection of photo-mechanical colour separation this process became largely obsolete. However, with a skilled operator it could never be entirely replaced. I know of one or two contemporary artists who have used this technique very successfully, but it takes great patience and much practice.

In England towards the end of the nineteenth century there were two artists called the Beggarstaff Brothers (James Pryde and Sir William Nicholson). Their work included posters for the theatre, which were enormous in size and were executed with stencils. They were hand printed and of relatively small runs. The great demand for their work reflects their brilliance at designing for the stencil. They used few colours and these were subdued, yet the impact made was incredible. Their work remains as a climax to the art of stencil designing in Europe.

The following incident provides a further link in the history of silk-screen printing. Some years ago in Cornwall a friend brought to me a box which he had found in an attic. On the lid of this wooden box was printed the name of Edison with several patent numbers. Inside, some jars of ink and a rubber roller could be seen. After these had been lifted out, what remained was a heavy metal plate, to the side of which was hinged a wooden frame, stretched across with silk. A printed label on the inside contained the information that this was an office duplicator— a forerunner of the kind of machine now manufactured by Gestetner and Roneo. But it really was a portable silk-screen printing press made up in typical Victorian brass and boxwood style. Where this fits into the history of screen printing I do not know; but I am certain that that kind of printing which became an office duplicator is as much a part of silk-screen printing as anything else I have so far mentioned; and you will see later that I treat this branch of the technique as a normal screen process.

From the practical point of view the great distinction of the screen process when compared to other techniques is its economic use of both space and machinery. For example with a portable unit one can make an imperial multi-coloured print in an average size kitchen, without much trouble. Not that this is ideal or even recommended—there will normally be a larger area available.

Another distinctive feature is the variety of surfaces that can be printed on—glass, plastic, wood, canvas, fabrics, and of course the almost limitless range of papers. The only requirement initially is that the surface be flat, although even three-dimensional surfaces can be printed. This, however, involves complex machines and is generally only undertaken by specialists. The general scope of the technique is vast, as can be verified by examining the variety of its commercial applications. Apart from printing fabrics and posters it is used on plastics that are subsequently vacuum formed (see pp. 61–3) in making printed circuits, transfers for pottery, and in glass etching where extreme accuracy is necessary such as for speedometer dials, and many other uses.

I shall deal solely with studio technique, giving details of the techniques that I have used and of some that I have myself developed. I shall emphasize the use of the process by the artist and avoid purely commercial methods which more often than not involve a highly skilled operator. Whilst there must be people who want the qualities and finishes of the commercial studios, I think it only reasonable to point out that the way in which a job is broken down and dealt with by various specialists in a commercial studio is very different from a single operator dealing with every aspect of the studio process. This should be borne in mind when looking at prints, whether they are posters or the work of some of the fine studios to be found both in this country and elsewhere.

Some of the drawbacks of the process should be noted at this stage. They stem mainly from the mesh of the screen itself. For the artist the main limitation of the process is the degree of detail obtainable. Silkscreen is regarded widely as a coarse technique when compared to a process such as lithography, and with some justice.

The lithographic plate can carry a larger area of ink film than the equivalent open area of the silk screen, and the grain of the plate is non-mechanical whereas that of the silk weave is very mechanical. This allows a far more natural tonal gradation with litho than with silkscreen. There are means of getting over this in screen printing, but it must be noted that it is a particular problem of the technique. The result of this is that you are dealing with strong contrasts, lacking in tone. If you want to obtain the effect of a chalk drawing or a fine wash, you do not normally use screen printing for it. Another problem peculiar to screen printing is that oil-based inks tend to leave a thick layer of ink. Whilst this can sometimes be an advantage, the danger of cracking with age is a problem, and a thin layer of ink is preferable.

This can only be achieved with practice.

These are the main drawbacks, which are not, however, insurmountable. The typical advantages of a screen print are its large areas of flat colour, sharpness of edge, brilliance of colour, in opaque as well as transparent ink, a mobility of image, quick colour changes, and general speed both in setting up a print and in taking the edition. As with most other techniques, the limitations are made by the individual artist. In other words one man's freedom is another man's limitation.

CHAPTER 2

The Screen and other Equipment

In describing the materials and equipment necessary for the silk-screen process I here assume that the operator wants to print at imperial size using more than one colour and with an edition run of forty plus. I am also assuming that he wishes to establish an autographic image. Photo-stencil is dealt with later but equipment described in this chapter will basically serve all the processes that I shall deal with.

BASE The base (the equivalent of the bed of a press) must be smooth and solid. The ideal surface is formica mounted on marine-plywood or block-board. This is resilient, easy to keep clean, not inclined to warp and virtually as smooth as glass. It will take registration marks which can if necessary be easily removed. Alternatives are plain plywood with a coating of shellac (button polish) or blockboard with the same coating. Plate glass can be used, but this besides being expensive is fragile. Any surface that is inclined to bend, such as battened hardboard, will be useless, since the pressure which is exerted by the squeegee will be lost in the bending of the board. According to the amount of use it will be put to the base can either be independent (like a drawing board which can be stored separately), or it can be a table top with permanent fixtures.

FRAME The screen frame on which the silk or its equivalent is stretched and which in turn carries the stencil must be strong enough to take the considerable strain of the stretched fabric. Frames can be bought already made up; and although these are an additional expense, they are to be recommended if the operator's carpentry is untrustworthy. Wooden frames are normal: metal frames are generally only used for machine printing. When building a frame select a wood that will not normally warp: although beech is excellent, it is difficult to obtain and any semi-hard wood will do. Soft wood will usually bend within the

Fig. 2
Three joints that can be used in making frames. *Left to right:* Butt and end joint supplemented with two dowel rods for greater strength. Mitre joint glued and nailed with corrugated fasteners. Overlapping joint glued and screwed

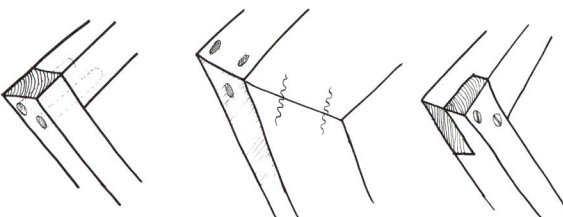

12

year and render the frames difficult or even impossible to use. Use $1\frac{1}{2}'' \times 2\frac{1}{2}''$ wood for the imperial size frame. The inside measurements of this would be $26'' \times 36''$. At least four must be allowed for the printing area.

The best joints to be used for the construction depend very much on the maker's skill. Mitre joints are often used although butt and end joints with dowell rods are easier to make and possibly stronger. To make sure that the frame lies flat, clamp the cut pieces with G-clamps to a firm flat surface. Any drilling or screwing can then be carried out and the adhesive left to dry. Rub down the completed frame with glass paper to get rid of any splinters and round off the outer edge on the side that will be the lower. This will greatly ease the stretching of the fabric. It is suggested that at least four screens be made, and that on completion they are left with heavy weights on top for 24 hours. This will help to ensure that they are flat. A smaller frame will be useful for test purposes, and for work of an experimental nature.

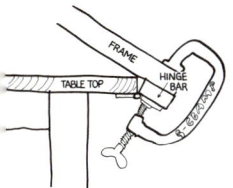

Fig. 3
Cross-section of a useful method of attaching frame to table

ATTACHMENT OF FRAME TO BASE

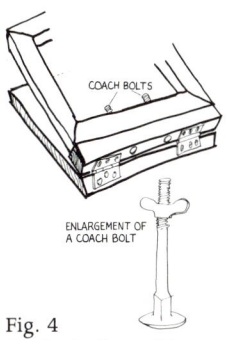

Fig. 4
Method of attaching frame to base using coach bolts

Next attach the frame to the base so that it can move up and down and will always fall in exactly the same position. Also see that it is reasonably easy to detach from the base for quick screen changes, cleaning, etc. A simple way is to hinge a strip of wood at one end of the base. The screen is then attached by two G-clamps. Another method is to use parliament hinges, which consist of two parts that slot together. But they have a tendency to slip which makes registration unreliable. A series of wooden notches can be made on both the base and the screen so that one drops into the other, but the problem is then what to do with the screen when replacing the wet print. Another way is to have a piece of wood permanently hinged to one end of the screen with a corresponding pair of holes drilled in it and in the base through which coach bolts can be placed.

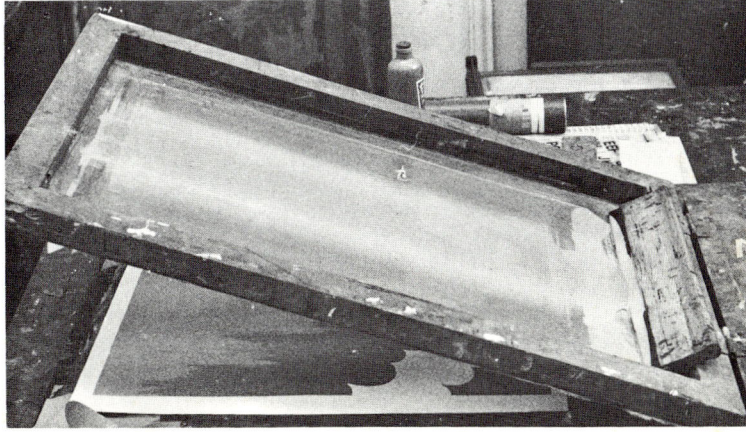

Fig. 5
Simple hinged frame unit

If there is enough space and a more permanent set-up is desired I would recommend instead of G-clamps a design developed some years ago by B. Sharpe that meets all these demands and has further advantages. It is a parallelogram on a table base. Two heavy bars of wood forty inches apart are secured to the underside of the table projecting eight inches on either side. (These bars can be bolted so that if necessary the press can be dismantled.) Pieces of planking each measuring six by twenty-four inches are attached to the bars with two hinges. These four legs should be hinged so that they will readily swing in an arc above the table top. The front set of legs is now joined together by a piece of wood the same size as those used for frames; again the joins are made with hinges; and the same process is repeated for the back pair of legs. You should now have two bars passing across the top of the table connecting the two sets of legs. Then place two pieces of wood between

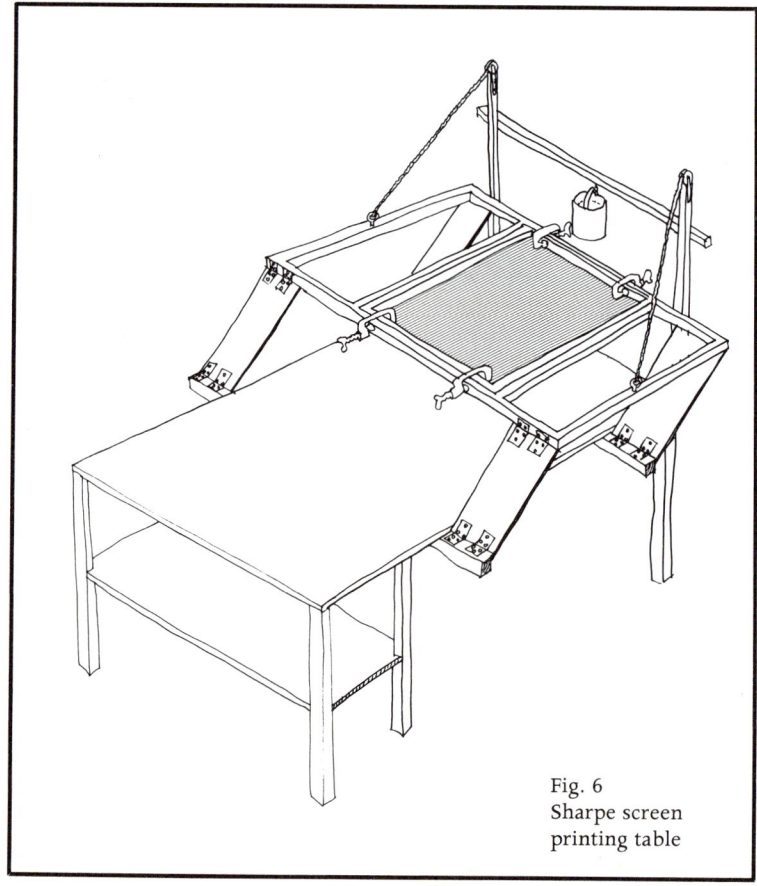

Fig. 6
Sharpe screen printing table

these two bars and parallel to the sides of the table. Again use wood of the same dimension as in the frames and screw these to the bars, having previously placed a frame on the top of the table in order to get the exact size. When these two bars are in position you should have a master frame in which the screens can be placed quickly and accurately for printing by means of G-clamps, one on every side. The frame so attached will rise in an arc from the table top, and always remain horizontal, thereby preventing the ink from running down the screen whilst paper etc. is being replaced on the base board. It will also give the operator far more room since the screen can be swung right away from the printing area.

To make a counterweight, fix one or two vertical bars at the far end of the table, and with the tops at least three feet above it. Fix pulleys on these with rope or cord passed over them to screw-eyes in the master frame. The cord is attached to pass over the bars with a weight tied to the other end so that more can be added or subtracted. This particular press has many other advantages, as for example when used for off-set silk-screen techniques.

SCREEN MATERIALS   With a base to print on and a frame to stretch the fabric on, next choose your screen material. There is a variety of available fabrics in a number of grades and I will deal with each separately: organdie, silk, nylon, terylene, and metal meshes. Each has its own characteristics.

Organdie
This is a cotton fabric which complies with the fundamental requirements of the process, although it is not manufactured primarily for this purpose. It is a coarse-mesh material used in dressmaking and is readily available in most large drapery stores. The quality varies slightly but this does not matter as a screen is not expected to last very long. Its main disadvantage is that it scarcely possesses enough strength for obtaining a well stretched screen. And since it is coarse it is unsuitable for the majority of screen techniques. Its chief value is that it is cheap and expendable, thereby providing a good screen for experiments and for the beginner.

Silk
Of all the fabrics available this is the most used. Its popularity is well founded. Screen-printing silk is very different from that normally used in dressmaking. It is pure silk with a high tensile strength and each of the several weaves has an open mesh. These weaves are named and graded from fine to coarse mesh. Silk bolting cloth (a general term) was originally intended (and is still used) for the sifting of flour, starch, and sugar. Although it did not come originally from Como in Italy it

was so widely manufactured there that it is now called como silk. It is this como silk which is used by virtually every screen printer, since it will do the greatest variety of jobs. There are over fifty different grades, which vary in mesh and in weight. A genuine como silk weave is one where an interlocking twist is given at each intersection of the warp and the weft, thus preventing the threads from closing up. Closed-up threads would prevent the easy passage of ink and be useless for this process. There are two basic como-silk weaves: full-gauze and half-gauze. In the full-gauze the threads are interlocked at each intersection, and in the half-gauze at every other intersection. These weaves withstand all the stretching involved in screen printing, plus the drag of the squeegee and the rub of cleaning. The grades of silk are based on the amount of twists in the yarn. There are four in all, standard, single x, double x and triple x. In addition to this the sizes vary with the number of meshes to the square inch. These start at 0000 which has 18 meshes to the square inch (the coarsest available) and continue to 25 with 200 meshes to the square inch.

Screen printers use between 4 and 20 of these sizes. The general rule is, the coarser the mesh the heavier the deposit of ink. The main factor in choosing a particular size or material will be the technique to be employed, which in turn depends on the quality of the image desired. Grades x and xx in sizes between 2 and 20 are the most readily available.

Nylon

This is a man-made monofilament (that is not spun as a yarn but extruded as setting liquid threads). Because it is woven like silk it is called como nylon. However, as this is a monofilament, twisting it at the intersection would not bring about the interlocked state desired: it is therefore heat sealed (welded) at the intersections. The threads chosen for this purpose are less elastic than normal nylon threads, since it is important that the screen should not distort when it is carrying a stencil. Nylon is used widely in commercial printing studios where long runs are needed. But silk is much the same price and for normal studio work its life is about the same. Nylon is not recommended for use with water-based inks since these tend to slacken the weave. Also there are certain inks which contain strong solvents which will attack the threads; but these are mostly used only by the specialist and generally carry instructions as to whether or not they are safe with nylon. An advantage that monofilament threads have over spun threads is the ease of cleaning, but a disadvantage is that certain photoprinting techniques cannot always be used with nylon. The sizes of nylon are numbered differently from those of silk but are still based on the same system with 110nn being approximately equivalent to 11x or 11xx silk.

Terylene
Again this is monofilament and like nylon is a relatively recent introduction. It is cheaper than nylon or silk and has great durability. For the studio worker virtually the only drawbacks to using terylene and nylon are that some specialized inks will attack the thread. Terylene, like nylon, is easy to clean and like all the materials mentioned so far, with the exception of organdie, it will last a considerable length of time if looked after.

This of course depends on the operator; a screen can take a multitude of images, and if it is thoroughly cleaned each time and not ripped it will last well over a year. With man-made fibres such as terylene a far greater uniformity of weave can be achieved. This allows for a greater degree of accuracy, although for most requirements the improvement is minimal. Terylene is recommended for use on large screens since it is dimensionally more stable than the previously described fibres. Although most substances will adhere to it, it is advisable to check the patent stencil materials since some will not adhere readily to terylene.

Metal meshes
These are made from stainless steel wire and are of a specialized use, where extreme accuracy is required or where an ink would unduly damage the previously described fibres. For example, ceramic inks (which tend to be abrasive) are used with metal meshes; heavier deposits of these inks are also generally required and so the stronger meshes are needed. Metal meshes are not recommended for general use as they are easily dented.

The meshes so far described are generally available on the market at present. However, there are many other materials which at first glance would not appear to be of any use to the screen printer. One such material was discovered by the students of the textile department of Camberwell School of Art: lace curtaining; it would be of no use as it is to the manufacturer, it is nevertheless worthy of note by the artist.

Throughout this book I suggest that the operator experiment not only for the reasons already given but because screen printing is still a very young process and as such has a long development ahead. Sooner or later the industry will get away from the idea of woven meshes and take to matted meshes which have some advantages. For example, there is a matted fabric available for dressmaking that can also be used for screen purposes; it is called 'Vilene'. The finer versions of this plastic fibre are the only ones of any use for screen printing. Stretching presents some problems as it is inclined to tear and I would not recommend the beginner to try it. The main advantage (other than economic) is that in a matted fabric the mesh is irregular. This allows for a better tonal gradation than regular woven meshes.

STRETCHING A SCREEN

The stretching procedure varies slightly with the kind of fabric being stretched. Organdie is not very strong and is inclined to tear. Silk, nylon, and terylene can take considerable strain: they will not tear unless they are jerked.

A piece of fabric is cut larger than the frame and then attached to one of the shorter sides and pulled tight. (It is advisable to try to get the mesh aligned as near as possible to the frame.) Now attach it to one of the longer sides pulling this time away from the first attached side. Next tighten against the second long side.

At this stage (with one side still unattached), if it is silk that is being stretched it must be dampened all over with water and a sponge, and then left for a few minutes. This is not necessary with other fabrics but dampening ensures a very taut finish with silk. It is attached to the last side with gentle but firm tension.

The essential point in stretching is to get the fabric as tight and even as possible. The most convenient means of attachment is stapling, but drawing pins can be used, although these are more laborious to fix and not so efficient.

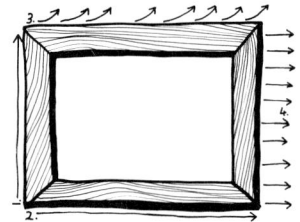

Fig. 7
Stretching a screen using a staple gun; arrows indicate direction of pulling

There are machines available for stretching screens. Most of them use adhesives for attaching the fabric to the frame. Their cost restricts them to larger establishments.

The next stage is to seal the edges to prevent ink from seeping between frame and fabric. This is done with gummed paper and shellac varnish. Cut and stick a band of gummed paper to either side of the screen and all round the edge, to cover part of the frame and at least two inches of the screen itself. When this is dry, stick a strip of banner linen on the inside of the screen to cover the join between fabric and frame. Banner linen is a tough fabric treated with starch. It is attached with gum arabic and when dry it is coated with shellac varnish. This will make it resistant to the solvents in the ink and aid cleaning the screen.

A screen will last well if it is properly looked after (that is, properly cleaned without strong caustic agents or abrasives). When it becomes necessary to re-stretch the screen the fabric is torn off and the frame cleaned up. Remove all staples or drawing pins.

THE SQUEEGEE   This is of prime importance; it is the implement with which the print is taken. If there is any skill involved in normal screen printing then it is in the use of the squeegee, which should always be kept in the best condition. The main requirement is that the blade be kept sharp to minimize the effort involved in pulling a print. However it may be otherwise shaped, the blade must not be curved since the whole of the edge must be in contact with the screen when drawn vertically across it.

The rubber for the blade can be obtained in three different grades (soft, medium, and hard). For normal printing on paper a medium grade rubber is sufficient. But where the thinnest ink film is required with maximum sharpness of image a hard rubber will be found more efficient. Soft rubber would be used for printing on paper with water-based inks or where a heavier deposit of ink is required. If heavy deposit inks are required there are generally more efficient means of obtaining them.

A plastic blade (which at this stage is still not fully developed) is also obtainable. Its main advantage is its durability, but it tends to harden with age and eventually becomes unworkable. A squeegee is usually set in a wooden handle although some handles are made of metal (mainly for use with various patent machines). Probably the best hand squeegees available are of composite construction, allowing the blade to be renewed or turned with ease. They consist of a profiled piece of wood with two detachable side plates made of alloy. When these plates are in position they lock the blade against the wood. Normally the blade is set in a wooden channel and screws, passing through the wood and rubber, hold them together. Perfectly adequate cheap squeegees can be made quite easily with three pieces of wood, one of which is as thick as the rubber, placed together like a sandwich. There are a number of effective variations and if the final fixing can be done so that the rubber can be removed and replaced at ease this will obviously be better still.

Fig. 8
Various types of squeegees in section. *Left to right:* Home built, using three pieces of wood to make the cross-section shown, into which is placed the rubber strip. Composite type with rubber strip held by two metal plates either side of a wooden handle. Grooved and shaped wooden handle. Machine type made of metal.

Maintenance of a squeegee is of the utmost importance, and care should be taken to see that it is kept sharp. There are a number of gadgets for easy sharpening. The most efficient is the one used by woodworkers which has a continuous band of sandpaper rotating at high speed; the squeegee to be sharpened is placed against this at right angles to the moving sandpaper. Alternatively, a sandpaper block can be used, with the squeegee clamped to a bench, but make sure that the final surface is level. It is suggested that experiments for squeegees be made with various materials. I have known heavy card toughened with shellac to be sufficient where the printing area was rather small. After all, the blade merely pushes the ink across (and at the same time through) the mesh.

I have no doubt that in time the squeegee will change drastically, and perhaps become a roller or rollers. Certainly one of the advances made recently is the one-hand-action squeegee. This allows an operator to print a far larger sheet size than before and probably with a distinct improvement in quality. The principle is that a metal squeegee is clamped to a bar, one end of which is attached by runners to another bar, parallel to the printing frame. This allows the squeegee to move up and down across the frame. As this bar extends beyond the edge of the frame the operator can hold it down and work the squeegee by walking along the frame. These units can be bought separately, although they are usually marketed with a complete printing table and vacuum unit.

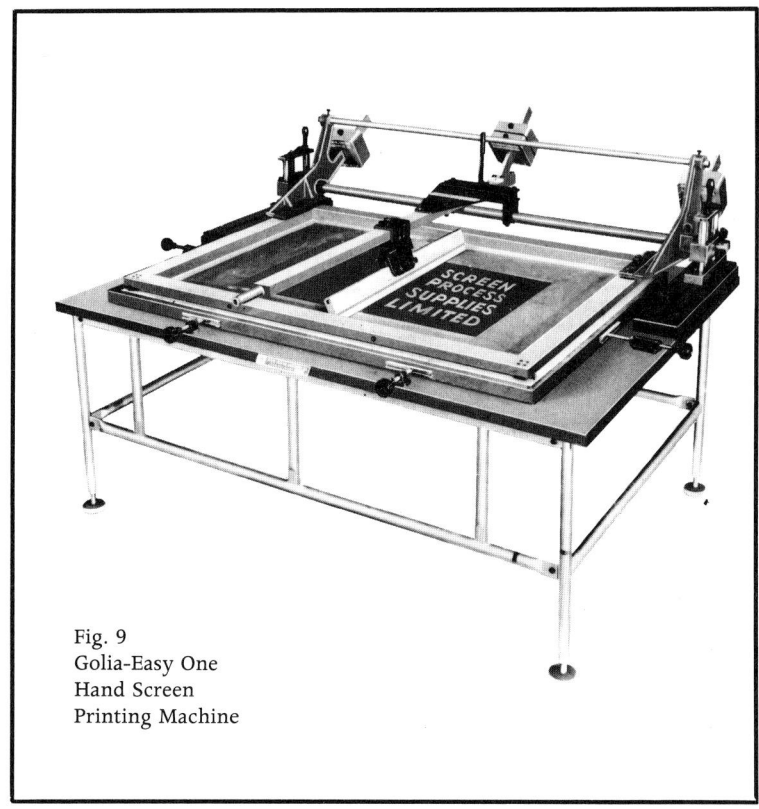

Fig. 9
Golia-Easy One
Hand Screen
Printing Machine

DRYING RACKS   One of the problems with screen printing is that when it is operating correctly, the delivery of wet prints is rapid, so that it is often difficult to dry them without damage (particularly in a confined space). A simple hanging rack with clothes pegs can be made to carry up to 100 prints. This is particularly useful where there is a high ceiling, since the loaded rack can be safely hoisted to the ceiling by pulley. Another rack can be made with wooden frames across which is stretched wire netting. The wet print is placed face upwards on the first of these and another rack placed over this in readiness for the next print. This method is particularly useful if the bottom frame is attached to a trolley, so that the completed stack can be moved to a more convenient position for drying. The time a print takes to dry will depend initially on the kind of ink used; but since most inks dry by evaporation the process can be speeded up. A good circulation of dry fresh air helps, but a hot air fan is probably better if the air current is not too strong or too hot.

A large number of prints will give off fumes so that it is advisable to move them away as soon as possible. The main object of the rack is to keep wet prints safe since they are particularly easy to damage. It

Fig. 10
Using a drying rack
for wet prints

should be immediately adjacent to the printing area. If this is not possible then some means should be devised for carrying prints quickly to the rack. The act of printing is very much a rhythm and the degree of technical success when printing an edition largely depends on maintaining this rhythm. If the operator has to keep walking several quite unnecessary steps after each print then he will find it almost impossible to maintain the level of absorption needed to produce good work. This will require a lot of thought and many adjustments to the positions of the rack and of the clean paper storage will be necessary. Often in commercial houses a printer will have two people working with him, one to feed him with paper and one to take the wet print away. Under such circumstances incredible speeds can be achieved, but also, what is more to the point, a high standard of printing can be maintained, since the printer has no interruption whatsoever, and this for long runs is of great importance.

Other items that will be needed are: a stapler, which is mainly used in stretching the screens but has many other applications; a pair of canvas pliers for stretching screens; steel straightedges, palette knives, scissors, etc. An endless supply of old rags, newspapers, and cardboard is absolutely vital. Cardboard is cut into small rectangles and used for scraping surplus ink from the screen when printing is over. Reels of gummed paper 2" and 4" in width and Sellotape will also be needed.

CHAPTER 3

Ink and Paper

The study of ink and paper for the printing industry would be as vast an undertaking as their manufacture. It is difficult for the artist to gain the essential information concerning the materials he is likely to need partly because the authors of the more erudite books on paper or ink seem to expect the reader to be a chemist with an honours degree. This often means that an artist is denied valuable information to the detriment of everyone involved. The artist will also possibly be daunted by the sheer number and specialized nature of the manufacturers' leaflets. These will have, for the most part, little to do with what he sees as his own needs. I shall not try to bridge the art/technological gap in this chapter, but merely give some idea of the materials that artists use.

INK Any screen ink has some basic requirements, if it is to go onto paper, glass, etc. It must have enough body not to flow unduly on the screen and seep through areas where it is not required. The pigment must be ground finely enough to pass through any mesh without clogging the screen. Because so much ink is used in this process (compared to others) it must be cheap, non-toxic and as odour-free as possible.

There are four main kinds of screen ink: (1) oil-based, the ones most likely to be used by the artist; (2) cellulose-based, some of the cheapest made; (3) water-based, with some marvellous qualities; and (4) plastic inks. (Some other inks are used with screen printing that strictly speaking do not come under these headings, for example ceramic ink, which is used for the printing of glass and pottery.)

Oil-based inks
These are widely used, since they have durability and permanence. They consist fundamentally of pigment, driers, and binding medium, which can be synthetic resin or boiled linseed oil. Manufacturers can offer many finishes—matt, gloss, super gloss, super matt, and eggshell to name a few. However, what should be looked for is covering power. This is generally good with most screen inks since the film is thick. As a general rule the finer the pigment is ground the better the coverage and the sharper the definition. Cheap ink is often padded out with substances such as alumina hydrate, which make it more transparent and the printed surface is also liable to crack after six months.

Most manufactured ranges of oil-based ink have a transparent version so made that it can be extended or made even more transparent. This should be used judiciously since it tends to crack. However, by using it, the artist can achieve effects that are only possible by overprinting and by combining transparent with opaque colours.

Screen ink should have a matt finish. Varnish can always be added to produce a gloss ink; but it is almost impossible to reduce a gloss ink to a matt one.

It is essential to know the solvent to be used. Anything other than white spirit can involve the expense of special thinners and cleaners. Most oil-based inks are solvent in white spirit, although some recently introduced demand a more specialized and generally stronger solvent. Keep to one range when using different coloured inks to ensure that they will intermix: inks from different ranges might be incompatible. The following formula for an oil-based ink gives some idea of the proportion of ingredients:

White screen ink (Beck Koller formulation)	
Anastase	26·5
Precipitated chalk	15·0
Blanc fixé	12·5
Beckosol 9610 (50% solid)	46·0

The driers would be added to this and would amount to 1%. The solvent for such an ink is white spirit.

Nitro-cellulose screen inks

Similar in make-up to oil-based inks, although the operator would notice a difference of smell. And here I must recommend caution: since some inks tend to give off injurious fumes adequate ventilation must be maintained at all times. White spirit will not always dissolve these inks, so cellulose thinners may have to be used, and these can be harmful to the skin. I do not recommend such ink for the single operator with limited space: although they are cheap, their drawbacks cancel out this advantage.

Water-based inks

Little used in the screen industry at the moment. Their advantages are limited and they set peculiar problems. But one of the distinct advantages for the artist is that they are the cheapest he is likely to find. To the best of my knowledge there is only one ink manufacturer who markets a true water-based ink, so anyone who wishes to work with them may have to make them himself. This can be an advantage since far more control can be obtained.

The basic ingredients are a gum to bind and stiffen the ink, plus pigment or dye. To deal with the gum first: there is a variety of gums that can be used, both man-made and natural. The following is a selection:

British Gum D: a man-made gum prepared by boiling in the proportion of 10 lbs. gum to one gallon of water.

'Meypro' Gum CRX: a man-made gum, easy to mix and store. The powdered gum is mixed with the water preferably with an electric mixer. The proportion is 1 lb. of gum to two gallons of water. Warm water will help the mix but boiling is not absolutely necessary.

Gum Tragacanth: a natural gum best obtained as a readily mixable powder. It can be made up and left over night to be stirred thoroughly the next day, after which it should be brought to the boil to be ready for use. The proportion is 7 lbs. gum to 10 gallons of water.

Gum Arabic: another natural gum used in lithography. The lumps of gum are soaked in water over night, then slowly brought to the boil with constant stirring. (It can also be obtained as a powder which is easier to mix.) The proportion is 4 lbs. of gum to one gallon of water. When this has finally cooled down strain before use.

The wallpaper pastes such as 'Polycell' can also be used (but if a lot of ink is to be made, buy it in bulk rather than piecemeal over the shop counter).

Any pigments can be used if they are finely ground. They are mixed with the prepared gum but may need extra water.

Water-based ink may dry on the screen. This can be avoided by adding a retarding substance such as glucose; but too much of this will result in tackiness.

Other colours that can be used with gum are the aniline dyes. A few of these are fugitives: dyes are water soluble, spirit soluble, and oil soluble. The latter are used for tinting oil-based inks. Some spirit soluble dye can be used for making water-based screen ink. The dye (which for the most part comes as a powder) is mixed in a separate container with water. The addition of a little methylated spirit will help, as this acts as a wetting agent. It must be realized that these dyes are extremely strong colouring agents and that only a little need be used to get the desired strength of colour. The thoroughly dissolved dye is then trickled into the gum and stirred well. It cannot be emphasized enough that the mixing must be thorough, otherwise the resulting prints will be streaky. There will be bleeding through any overprinting and this can sometimes be exploited.

The other major problem is that water-based inks tend to cockle and even shrink a thin printing paper. The only answer to this is to use a paper that is capable of absorbing the gum. On the other hand, the advantages of these inks are that (1) there is no build-up of ink on the surface of the paper which is such a normal characteristic of screen prints,

(2) softer and more subtle colours can be achieved, (3) cleaning with water is relatively easy and certainly cheap. Gum and dye inks are well worth investigating since their results are quite different.

Possibly one of the finest inks, if not the finest, ever made for screen printing that can be used by the artist is pigmented fabric ink; although it is not strictly speaking a water-based ink, water plays a large part in its make-up. Polyvinyl Acetate is the key (it can also be based on latex). This ink was developed for the fabric printing industry and has an interesting history which goes back to printing on silk. This at one stage was done by using such substances as albumen (egg white) and pigment, as opposed to dye. Once this had been printed and dried onto the fabric the albumen was coagulated either with steam or the fumes of acetic acid. There were variations on this method, but all depended on the principle that a liquid pigment carrying medium was later coagulated, so that the pigment it contained was held fast for most practical purposes. Thus (amongst other things) a metallic surface could be printed on fabrics, but although this was reasonably resistant to washing, etc., it left much to be desired in other respects. At this point a plastic such as Polyvinyl Acetate was used. This is soluble in water and will coagulate like albumen, but even then it is not perfect. However, if it is mixed with white spirit and water (the one to thicken, the other to thin) and a pigment is then added, and if this mixture is subsequently printed onto fabric (or paper) allowed to dry and then subjected to heat, the white spirit is evaporated and the p.v.a. is polymerized. This is a very effective form of coagulation. It means that a thermo-plastic has changed into a thermo-setting plastic, a change which is absolutely unalterable and is very permanent and stable compared to the binding agents employed in oil-based ink or cellulose ink. The final surface is eggshell in quality and not raised at all.

The heat treatment used for fabrics is not necessary with paper prints, since these are not going to be washed and the phenomenon described will take place over a longer period of time by natural evaporation. A little heat will certainly help in the early stages but certainly no more than that used to dry any other printing inks. There are several ink manufacturers who market inks based on this principle: some are already made up while others have to be mixed by the operator when required. Like the water-based inks already described, this ink is completely odourless. The depth of colour and general freshness with these pigment printing inks makes them highly desirable.

Plastic inks
It would be impossible to attempt a description of all the plastic inks available. There are as many inks as there are plastics; and most of them are for specialized printing onto particular plastic surfaces. If the

operator wishes to print on a particular plastic he can rest assured that there is an ink suitable for it. As the plastics are often machined or formed in some way after the printing, an even more specialized ink is called for, capable of withstanding this treatment. For example, an ink for printing onto acrylic sheeting would probably have pigment bound in an acrylic solvent or even some kind of liquid acrylic, so that the bond between print and sheet is such that they become virtually one and the same substance without a join.

If subsequently the sheet of acrylic were to be vacuum-formed then this would present a whole new set of problems to the ink manufacturer. For example, there are inks made to print on a sheet of polystyrene before it is vacuum-formed. The ink film can be stretched a long way without sign of thinning. This means that the pigments in such an ink must have great covering power. The artist is advised to consult a manufacturer about any job that involves plastics.

Thermographic ink
An extremely interesting ink available on the market, which is manufactured for letterpress work but can be used for screen printing, is called thermographic ink. It is manufactured by Adana Ltd., for use with their machines, but does not really need any special equipment for small run work. It consists of a powder that comes in various grades and finishes. The quality peculiar to this product is that it prints in an embossed manner. The procedure is simple enough using any type of stencil and any type of mesh, and a water-based gum or a transparent extender base, normally in conjunction with oil-based ink, or any oil-based ink alone, except that the colour from the latter will affect the final result. When a print has been pulled, whilst it is still wet, dust on the thermographic powder liberally and then shake off the surplus. The print is then subjected to heat which makes the powder fuse and swell and set hard on cooling. The powder is a resin-based composition that comes in three different grades. The coarser grades are used for large flat areas and the finer grades for delicate work. The material is by and large colourless and will adopt the colour of the ink used. When heated and fused to the sheet it has a high gloss finish that to my knowledge is quite unique. It is strange that this has not been used in print making as it has a number of possibilities.

PAPER Unlike most other printing processes, screen printing can be done successfully on any kind of paper. In fact one can go far beyond the limits of paper; for example, wood in sheet form can be readily printed. The final quality required depends more on the surface, and to a lesser extent on the kind of ink chosen. There is a great variety of papers available to the artist; most are machine made, and only a few hand made. Whether they are hand or machine made they will consist basically of the same substance; a cellulose fibre of vegetable origin, to which will have been added gelatine or size and inorganic white fillers for opacity. The strength of a paper lies in the length of the fibre. Cellulose fibres are obtained mainly from wood, rag, straw, sawdust, bamboo, hemp, jute, and esparto grass. Each source produces its own kind of paper or card and general range of quality. High quality papers are made of rag or cotton waste which is boiled with a dilute caustic soda and subsequently bleached. Low grade papers and boards are made from wood, straw, and esparto grass, the cellulose from which is often obtained chemically with acids, but this is not always an economic alternative to mechanical pulping; and the paper so made has a relatively short life and should be avoided by any artist who wishes his work to last longer than a few years.

Here are some papers of various fibre mixture that the artist might come across:

Antique papers. These are normally cream coloured and can be matt finished or rough surface. They are made from deciduous wood or straw pulp and have a wire watermark of netted or long parallel lines.

Art papers. These are coated with china clay to ensure an exceptionally smooth finish, so much so that they appear glazed. Made from wood pulp and mainly used for off-set photo-litho and reproduction work in general.

Cartridge papers. Strong, semi-bleached or unbleached papers made from jute, manila, and kraft pulp. These are used to a considerable extent by artists. Some are made from wood pulp and most contain size of some sort.

Litho papers. Made from esparto or straw and generally excellent for silk-screen printing. They contain little or no size and do not curl. There is a great variety of finishes from rough to smooth, and also of whiteness: some are super-white.

M.G. poster papers. These are bleached sulphite papers which are highly glazed on one side and rough on the other. The rough surface is to give better adhesion to hoardings, since posters are mostly printed on this paper.

Parchment papers. These are similar to cartridge papers. They contain size as well as some starch. Creamy in colour they can have a rough or smooth finish.

Newsprint. This is the cheapest printing paper available. It is made from wood pulp, contains no size and is only used for proofing up in the studio.

Tissue paper. These are fine strong papers made from rag and hemp for best quality, with cheaper grades made from wood pulp.

Any of these papers, and many more that have not been mentioned, can be used for screen printing. The screen technique is not particularly affected by the absorbency, roughness, or hardness of paper, although the qualities do to some extent determine the kind of ink to be used. For example, it could be said that an oil-based ink is best used with an absorbent paper, since most of the ink would be absorbed and there would be little or no build-up on the surface. A surface build-up of oil-based ink is not always desirable since the gradual evaporation of plasticizing agents leaves the ink film in a brittle condition. However, this very build-up quality can be used to great effect, so there can be no absolute rules as to which paper is best. With all but those inks that incorporate dyes, the paper fibres are first coated with pigment and any ink builds up into a surface film. In inks that are dyes, the colouring agent imbues and the binding gum coats the fibre. Once the moisture has evaporated there is little bulk left and the ink is stable.

For most work that is to go into galleries hand-made (or mould-made) papers are used since these can take handling much better than cartridge. They do not crease so easily and will take the weight of ink without curling. Most of these papers are sized and can be obtained with a variety of surfaces. Filter paper (as used in chemistry) can be used as a substitute for handmade paper, although it does not handle well and needs considerable care. There are many Japanese papers available in this country and they have a wide range of qualities. The softer white papers which often come in dimensions well above imperial are unsized, and need great care in handling. The decorative Japanese papers can be used to print on successfully but are often too overpowering for the printed image. Difficult at the moment to obtain, but well worth investigation, are the plastic papers. These are matted fibres of various plastics. There is also a plastic paper available that is matted then heat welded. This is extremely strong, washable, and drapes like a fabric. It is quite obvious that such papers will be increasingly found on the market. They will prove invaluable to the artist who wants to send his work round the world in small quantities as they can be washed and ironed by each gallery on receipt.

Non-fibrous, unabsorbent surfaces, such as metal, can be printed, but a combination of specialized inks and some after-treatment is needed for permanence. There are some surfaces that are virtually impossible to print on. One such surface is polythene, but then this is used to good advantage by transfer printers who use polythene as a temporary carrying surface.

CHAPTER 4

The Stencil I

The essence of the silk-screen process is the stencil; and there is a great variety in the stencils that can be used. In selecting a particular kind of stencil, the determining factor is the sort of image desired: each stencil gives a distinctive finish as well in the actual form of the image itself. Each process embodies a particular way of thinking which the artist can only discover by use. It must therefore vary from individual to individual. But before I deal with making a stencil let me describe the printing action.

PRINTING   Taking a print or proof is fundamentally the same for all the processes that will be described. If there is any skill required it is in pulling the print, although, compared to the skills demanded by other printing techniques, it is comparatively easy and can be mastered reasonably quickly. I would suggest that at first a stencil of the simplest kind is used, so that the problems met with are minimal. For example, print something that can be used as background for a number of further prints. Since there is little point in taking just a few pulls at this stage, try to pull as near to a hundred as possible. This will pay off, for not only will it give the operator a chance to come to terms with the actions of printing it will also teach him a lot about the general set-up. It will soon become obvious if the paper is kept too far from the printing table; whether the drying arrangements are sufficient and easy to get to; and many other points will arise that can only really be assessed under working conditions.

Having set the screen up ready for printing, made the appropriate stencil and put the first sheet of paper to be printed in place, make sure that there is sufficient ink ready prepared. This should be about a pint. (Do not worry about making too much as it can be easily stored and used again.) Charge the screen with ink at the end furthest away from you (so that the initial pull will be towards you). The ink should be arranged in a sausage shape the width of the screen and on the masking NOT on the area to be printed (otherwise it will start to run through the mesh immediately and cause trouble). Take a squeegee wider than the image by at least an inch at each side and put it down beyond the band of ink before pulling it towards you. The main factors that will govern the results you will obtain are the angle at which the squeegee is held and the amount of pressure applied. The angle of the blade should be close to 45 degrees; if it is too vertical it will not be able to transmit the pressure applied evenly across the width. On the other hand if the angle is too

Fig. 11
Charging the screen with ink

Fig. 12
Two views of pulling a print

acute then virtually no pressure is applied and the result will be that the ink is neither pushed through the mesh nor pulled across the screen. The main indication that the pull has been good is that the texture of the mesh is readily discernable. If the mesh has partly disappeared under a thick layer of ink then this indicates that the ink, instead of being pushed through the mesh, has simply been left on top, and a second pull in the opposite direction will be necessary, for if the screen were left in this clogged state the ink would start to permeate the screen of its own accord. This would cause trouble later and should be rectified fairly quickly.

The only useful comparison with the action of squeegeeing I know is scraping off varnish from a table top with a razor blade. There is one particular angle at which the maximum amount of varnish is removed. If the razor is too upright it only scratches the surface; if it is too flat then nothing happens at all. The same applies to the squeegee, although I do not suggest that as a preliminary you should go and scrape varnish from a table.

The movement of the blade should be smooth and continuous: do not stop on the printing area. If this happens the print taken will have a mark or ridge across it where the blade stopped. Also the ends of the blade should always be outside the printing area. If they are allowed to go across it, apart from leaving some areas unprinted they would also leave marks on the surface already printed.

At the end of the pull a slight reverse movement of the blade will help release surplus ink from it. The blade then can be placed at the further end of the screen resting against the frame. But take care not to drip ink across the screen as you go since this would leave marks on the print. You will have gathered that the printing area is vulnerable to many hazards even before it has been taken from the table but if perfect prints

Fig. 13
Removing a print after pulling

are required all these points must be taken note of.

Care must be taken, when lifting the screen to remove the print, particularly the first few times. If the screen is raised rapidly the vacuum created will partially pull the stencil away from the screen. This can cause an unpleasant change in the surface quality of the print in certain areas. Moreover if the screen is lifted too rapidly threads of ink may form and fall onto the unprinted areas. This can also damage paper-cut stencils.

The lifted screen must be propped up while the wet print is removed, and the next sheet of clean paper replaces it.

At first you may need to make two strokes of the squeegee, one up and one down. The stroke away from you will be weaker than that towards you but with practice this difference will be eliminated. But as the difference can cause slight variations in the quality of the prints I would suggest that to begin with all the prints are made with two strokes rather than one.

MAKING A STENCIL

1. Paper-cut

Probably the simplest stencil is cut paper. This is a good introduction to the technique and although simple can produce an almost infinite range of qualities. The paper should be as thin as possible, because the ink itself is an adhesive which will not be effective with a thick heavy paper. Furthermore a thin paper stencil is easier to cut, and the subsequent layer of ink, if printed correctly, will be correspondingly thin. This applies generally to all stencils; the thicker the stencil the heavier the deposit of ink. All ranges of mesh and sorts of material may be used. The process does not require any particular mesh characteristics. Since the ink is used to stick the stencil to the screen it should be stiffer than normal. There is no simple way of describing the exact consistency of ink required for each process, but as an approximation one can say it should be of the consistency of thin whipped cream.

The paper recommended for use as a stencil is Crystal Parchment. This is manufactured mainly for wrapping and is a tough translucent paper. Tracing paper is possible although not recommended since it has a tendency to expand when in contact with the ink. A waterproof paper should be used with water-based ink, or if this is not available one impregnated with an oily substance so that it is reasonably water-resistant. To prepare this, simply sponge or brush oil across the paper, making sure it is entirely covered and that no surplus oil is left to transfer itself to the first few prints.

Paper can be cut with a blade or scissors or simply torn. It will be found easier to work against a black background, cutting the stencil on a piece of black card, even though black may not be the colour being printed. This is in essence a negative process, that is, the torn or cut

fig. 14
Paper-cut made by a Polish peasant from *Wycinanta ludowa* by Jozef Grabowski, Warsaw: Vydawnictwo 1955, by kind permission of the publisher)

Fig. 15
Paper-cut stencil

Fig. 16 Paper-cut stencil on a darker ground

masking shapes represent white or non-printing areas. These need not be joined together: indeed the building up of a 'collage' may be the most convenient method. The image may then readily be moved and adjusted not only before printing but whilst printing. Having arrived at a statement which is to be printed, place the stencil under the screen. If the stencil consists of a number of loose pieces, then place the cardboard underneath at the same time. Lower the screen gently so that no loose pieces are disturbed. From here on the stencil is printed as previously described. If by raising the screen some parts of the stencil are dislodged, make sure there is enough ink on the pieces to hold them in place and put them back on the screen. Any necessary adjustment to the image can be carried out at this stage. The paper stencil can be moved about on the underside of the screen very easily and new pieces added by merely dabbing them with ink and pressing to the screen.

One of the more common faults that occur in printing is that of 'flooding', and paper-cut stencils are prone to this. Flooding is ink getting under the stencil and making a mark where none was intended. Bad flooding may even release the stencil from the screen. If it is not so bad that the whole image must be abandoned, the cause must be traced and dealt with.

(i) It may be that the screen is not stretched sufficiently. It will then buckle when a squeegee passes across and either the stencil will be temporarily released from the screen or double printing will occur on the return stroke and a certain amount of ink will get on the wrong side of the stencil: this can eventually build up enough to cause flooding.

(ii) Particles of grit near the edge can be another cause of flooding. A precaution is to brush the printing surface and the underside of the screen before printing: as a remedy gently peel off enough of the stencil to remove the particle.

(iii) If the ink is too thin it may run when the screen is resting at an angle and so pass through the mesh and cause a build-up of ink between it and the stencil.

2. Liquid Stencil

Of equal simplicity is the stencil applied as a liquid. Although this is not as flexible as the previously described technique it is nevertheless important. It consists of applying a liquid which becomes the stencil as it sets on the screen. The ideal liquid is one which dries quickly but is readily removed from the screen; and there is one manufactured that is called 'blue filler'. This is a water-soluble cellulose, coloured for convenience. There is also one called red filler, which is a lacquer soluble in methylated spirit. Glue size or gelatine can also be used, although they do take slightly longer to dry. (In selecting a liquid for a stencil, it is important to bear in mind the sort of ink that will be used for printing;

Fig. 17 Brush-on liquid stencil

Fig. 18 Sprayed-on liquid stencil

this should not damage the stencil. For example, if a water-based ink is to be used then obviously a stencil soluble in water is of no use.) The most straightforward way of using this process is to paint straight onto a clean screen remembering that you are masking out.

The work is carried out on the top of the screen so that it prints the same way round and not as a mirror image. Avoid globules of liquid as these not only take time to dry and are difficult to remove afterwards, but also may impair the print by increasing the deposit of ink around them.

It must be realized that the finer the mesh of the screen used, the finer the result—although delicacy is not a characteristic of this process. Coating the screen before use with starch and allowing it to dry will help towards a crisper image. The starch mixture should not be thick enough to block out the screen but just sufficient to coat the fibres. Any kind of material can be used and the ink can be thin since it is not here required as an adhesive.

A spray diffuser will also apply a stencil by fixing a variety of objects laid out on the screen. For example, the results are interesting if liquid is sprayed on string placed over the screen.

Small blocks such as potato cuts can be applied to the stencil. Paint the block with the liquid stencil and print on to the screen.

Liquid stencil can also be applied to glass, as one does with paint or ink for a mono-print, although a slightly heavier deposit of liquid stencil will be needed. Either coat a sheet of glass with stiff liquid stencil or paint the image upon the glass with any necessary adjustments. In order to transfer the image to the screen, place the glass beneath it and make sure it is everywhere in contact. A roller can be used if the liquid is stiff, but the image can easily be smudged if the liquid is too thin: it is then better simply to press the frame down without touching the mesh. Care must be taken in lifting the screen from the glass since the vacuum set up between them might dislodge the still wet stencil. Try some practice runs with this method in order to find the best consistency of liquid.

Another method is to block the screen completely with liquid stencil and allow it to dry. The stencil is then made by partly dissolving the blocking out liquid either with a brush and water or by using a weak gum. By lightly greasing the surface beforehand with turps substitue or paraffin, effects similar to lithographs can be obtained as the water breaks up on the greasy surface yet still bites.

All these methods are most successful when using blue filler as it readily dissolves in water and at the same time dries quickly. I would recommend the student to begin with this; it can be used with all except water-based inks, and is easy to remove from the screen both during painting and on completion. However, by experimenting, a perfectly

Fig. 19
Wax stencil

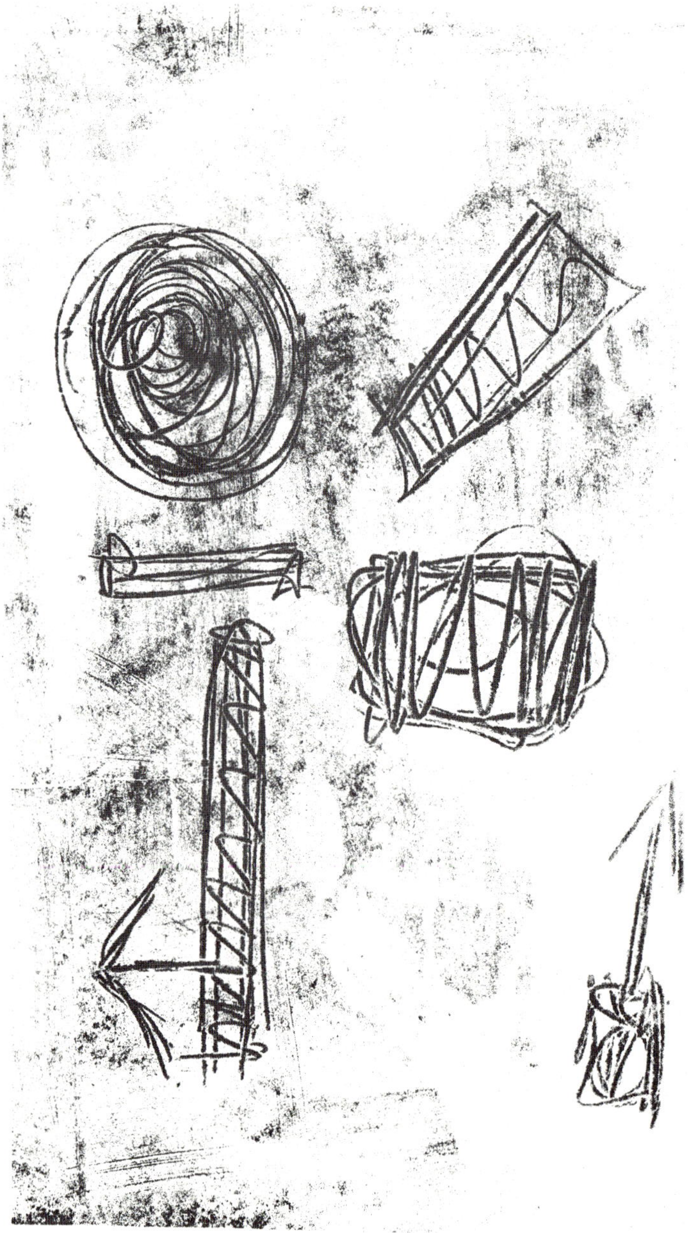

adequate liquid stencil preparation can be made from the following formula:

6 oz. of gelatine dissolved in 6 oz. of water; add 3 oz. of glacial acetic acid, 1½ oz. glycerine, ½ oz. alcohol and some colouring agent such as an aniline dye.

3. Wax Stencil

A simple stencil can also be made with wax. This has one major drawback: oil-based inks cannot be used since they will attack the stencil and eventually destroy it. Water-based inks have no effect on the stencil. The process is an adaptation of duplicator stencils that use wax. These can themselves be used and are readily available though they are limited in size for silk-screen printing. The aim is to get a blocked-out screen by using wax, which later can be pressed out in certain areas to create the stencil. Care must be taken in the preparation of the wax as it is necessary to melt it and it is highly inflammable.

Paraffin wax is the most usual type. Melt it, preferably in a double boiler, and add an equal volume of paraffin or white spirit away from the heat. The effect of adding paraffin is that when the wax re-sets it will be far softer and easier to manage on the screen. Whilst the wax is still in a liquid state, brush onto the screen completely blocking it out. This will semi-set immediately but will be too heavy a layer to work, so take a piece of stiff card that is not more than six inches long with a straight edge and, drawing this from side to side, scrape off the surplus wax from both sides of the screen. (It may be necessary to do this more than once, the idea being to get as thin a layer as possible.) This operation is carried out with the screen standing upright, for from now on anything that touches the screen may well take the wax out of the mesh, necessitating repair work. Check that the screen is completely blocked out by holding it up to the light. Paint out any pin holes with the wax (which if a double boiler has been used, will remain liquid for some time). Any such repairs should be similarly scraped down.

When the screen has been prepared, take a sheet of fibre-board or glass. Put this down on a working surface, placing the prepared screen on top but not in direct contact with the board. This is best achieved by fastening small pieces of card to the corners of the underneath side of the screen with drawing pins. The distance between the screen and the board should allow the screen to be pressed into contact. The image is drawn into the screen by pressing it onto the base with a ball-point pen, a match-stick, etc., so as to force out the wax. Drawing on a sheet of paper placed on top of the screen will not only make the work easier to see but will also take up wax from the screen on the under surface of the paper. The operator should take care not to rest his elbow or hand on the screen as this will damage the stencil. The image can be formed in

Fig. 20
Cross-section of cardboard attached to under side of the screen with a drawing-pin

many ways and with a variety of instruments; but avoid sharp instruments since they may pierce the screen. The delicacy of the results largely depend on the sensitivity of the wax layer: the thinner the layer the easier it will be to remove, and in consequence the drawing can be more detailed.

When the drawing is complete, leave for twenty-four hours in a cool part of the studio to allow the wax to set hard. Then print in the usual way, but remember not to use oil-based inks and to keep the ink thin. Use a fine mesh for this process. Although a coarse screen is possible the results will be far rougher since the image is intimately related to the mesh of the screen.

The half-and-half mixture described can be varied to suit the temperature of the studio: the more white spirit added the softer the wax will set and the longer it will take before it is safe to print from the screen. The addition of other waxes such as beeswax may give the stencil greater printing resilience, although it might also impair the sensitivity of the wax film. There can be no hard and fast rules as to quantities: one can only find the ideal mixtures by trial and error. The standard half-and-half mixture should be adequate but I advise the operator to try other mixtures and as many different instruments as possible.

4. Wash-out Stencil

The three basic processes so far described in this chapter are the simplest that I know of and, with the exception of the last, are used widely. They are classic examples of screen printing. Another standard technique once generally used but now not so much, is related to lithography. It is called the 'wash-out process' and in concept is very simple. A grease image is embedded in the screen and covered with a water-soluble glue; then the image is dissolved with turps, leaving a stencil of water-soluble glue.

The object is to get a masking-out image on the screen. This can be done with soft lithographic crayon. Place a screen on a flat surface and draw, pressing fairly hard so as to leave a heavy grease deposit. Remember this is a positive process so that what you draw will print. Alternatively a liquid wax can be used such as described in the previous process, consisting of half paraffin wax and half white spirit. A colouring agent of pigment or oil-soluble dye can be added to this to make it easier to see what you are doing. Paint the image on the top side of the screen which should not be in contact with the surface below but propped slightly at one end so that the wax does not run. When the image is complete, dust with french chalk. This will help it to resist the liquid glue of the next stage.

Blue filler is ideal for this but gelatine, glue, size, or gum arabic can

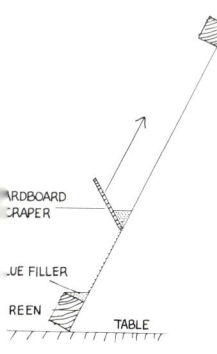

Fig. 21
Sectional diagram of blue filler being scraped across screen for wash-out process

be used, if the liquid is not too thick. It is better to give several thin coats than one heavy coat since this would make the subsequent removal of the grease or wax more difficult. This coating of the screen should be done with care. The screen is put upright with the top facing the operator. Apply the liquid with a large soft brush with long strokes across the screen as if applying a wash in watercolour. Do not overload the brush or the liquid will run down and through the screen. If this does happen then clean it off very carefully with a piece of blotting paper or tissue.

There is an alternative but more difficult method. The blue filler or gum (of a slightly stiffer consistency than would be needed for brushing) is poured in at one end of the screen which is tilted at a steep angle. The filler is scraped up the screen with a cardboard scraper until the whole area is covered. This method to some extent prevents globules forming on the wax areas. Leave the coated screen in a warm area of the studio and wait for it to dry. Then hold it up to the light to check for pin holes, and if any do exist give another coat. (It is advisable to give a second coat anyway to help build up the thickness of the stencil.) Then place the screen on top of some newspapers. Flood it with white spirit and rub the image with a rag to remove it and any liquid stencil that might have dried on it. A nail brush will remove any obstinate parts. Dry the screen and hold it up to the light to make sure that all that is left on the screen at this stage is a stencil made of blue-filler or whatever other filler was used. It will now be ready for printing with oil-based inks; but for water-based inks the stencil would need further treatment. In this case place the screen in contact with newsprint, brush or sponge a weak varnish across the whole of it, making sure that in the open areas varnish passes through onto the newspaper and does not remain in the screen. This is important, for if any varnish is left in the open areas it will block in the screen and thus defeat the whole intention.

There are variations on this wash-out technique many of which eventually destroy the screen if the stencil is made of a material which cannot be removed. Therefore, unless very long printing runs are intended a cheap screen material should be used. One such variation uses shellac and blue filler or a water-based gum. The image is painted on the screen with the water-based material, and alterations can be more easily made at this stage than with the wax method. When the image is drawn, allow it to dry thoroughly, and then check it against a light source to make sure that it is completely masked out. Once the image is established, shellac is either painted or scraped across the top side of the screen and allowed to dry. Again check this coating against the light for pin holes and if necessary give a second coat. The image is removed with *warm* water (hot water may damage the shellac coating). The water is applied to both sides of the screen. It dissolves the gum,

43

taking with it any dried shellac. It is then dried and is ready for use. Either oil- or water-based ink may be used with this shellac stencil. It will, however, be virtually impossible to remove the stencil from the mesh.

5. French Chalk

A further simple technique is carried out with french chalk. Its use is limited but might suggest other ideas. French chalk is spread out on a surface and drawn into like the sand maps in all the best Westerns. A screen is placed over the chalk image and oil-based ink squeegeed across. The ink picks up the chalk and combines with it to block the screen. But control over the image and the number of prints obtainable from such a screen are both limited. As with most of the other techniques described so far, the finer the mesh the finer the detail.

Fig. 22
French chalk stencil

Fig. 23
Profilm stencil

CHAPTER 5

The Stencil II

In this chapter I will deal with techniques that demand a little more skill from the operator but which provide greater scope.

HAND-CUT STENCIL PAPERS

The advantages of these are greater permanence and greater complexity. The stencil is more delicate and embedded in the screen so that a thinner ink may be used to give in turn that finer ink film. There are three different kinds on the market, and they vary in their method of adhesion to the screen as well as their use. But all three are fundamentally based on the same principle and incorporate the same idea.

A sheet of paper like heavy greaseproof paper is coated with a shellac setting liquid. To prevent this shellac permeating the backing sheet extremely fine tissue paper is first stuck down with a starch-like thermo adhesive that does not adhere too strongly and can be readily peeled off when heat is applied. When the setting liquid is applied it only permeates this tissue layer.

The most commonly used of the three films available is called *Profilm* and the setting liquid used in this case is a form of shellac. Place this transparent film over the design pinned to a board. All but the faintest marks will appear through it. A sharp cutting knife will be needed and the best type to use is that like a scalpel. The cutting will not need pressure if the blade is sharp. The film is cut through as far as the backing greaseproof paper, but the latter should not be cut as this would defeat one of the main advantages of the film. Before starting out on any big job try a few practice runs since some skill in cutting the film is needed. 'Islands' present no problems: for example the middle of an 0 should remain in place; but if some part of the film or an edge does happen to lift from the backing prematurely, a dab of petroleum jelly will keep it in place without in any way interfering with the process.

When a design is cut, no further adjustments are necessary or practicable before it is applied to the screen other than the act of stencilling and its final removal. To apply the design, some newspaper is placed in a substantial wad on a table. The backed film is placed on this, cut side uppermost. The screen is placed over it with the cut film in the appropriate position. A further sheet of newspaper is then placed on top of the screen to cover the total area of the film. A domestic iron, preferably one that incorporates a thermostatic control, is warmed to silk heat, and applied with normal ironing pressure to the screen, so that the heat begins to melt the shellac layer and make it tacky, and the pressure pushes the screen mesh into this tacky substance so that on cooling it will adhere to the screen.¹ One of the ways of checking whether the film has completely adhered is to see if it will anywhere reflect light. If there is any reflection or if a moiré pattern shows, this means that the film is insufficiently attached. A further check can be made by seeing if there is any slight change in surface colour, which may mean that some areas have not adhered sufficiently. Once the film has been stuck to the screen there only remains the backing to be peeled off. This operation should be carried out with some care, since if any parts have not stuck, the screen must be replaced on the newspaper and a second attempt made.

The backing sheet will come away more easily if one or two half-inch strips at the edge of the film could be lifted to give something to grip.

The stencil is finally removed by putting the screen on some newspaper and flooding it with methylated spirit. Another sheet is placed over the flooded screen and also soaked with methylated spirit and left for about fifteen minutes, by which time the shellac should have dissolved sufficiently for easy removal. Make sure that all trace of the shellac is removed since if it is allowed to dry again on the screen it will prove difficult to remove later.

Blue Film consists of a water soluble layer of cellulose, which is virtually the same as blue filler. The cutting of the stencil is the same as for profilm; the differences lie in the method of adhesion and the sort of meshes it will adhere to. Nylon and metal meshes cannot be used with blue film. The screen is damped with water just before adhesion so that when it is brought into contact the dampness will help to make the film tacky. The ironing is done as for profilm but the stencil is removed by washing since it readily dissolves in water. It is for this reason that oil-based rather than water-based inks must be used with it. Such films can be made cheaply at home. The necessary ingredients are shellac, beeswax, and cornstarch. Melt $1\frac{1}{2}$ oz. of beeswax in a double boiler. Add to this 8 oz. of shellac varnish and mix thoroughly. When completely mixed add one tablespoonful of cornstarch. Coat with the mixture a piece of heavy paper or card larger than the size of the image required. The coated sheet is left for 30 to 60 minutes until it becomes tacky. A sheet of tracing paper or its equivalent is then rolled on it so that it completely adheres without any air bubbles. Two coatings of shellac are then put on top of this sandwich, each coat being first allowed to dry. The sheet is then ready to use in the way described for profilm. The transparency of profilm will be achieved with this home-made version only if transparent backing such as tracing paper has been used, and its

---

[1] Care should be taken not to over heat the film in an attempt to speed up the adhesion process since this will only result in baking the film so that it can never be made to stick and will be wasted.

success will depend largely on the efficiency of the coating. This should be as even as possible and not too thick.

There are a number of advantages for the operator who makes his own film over the user of the orthodox manufactured film. He can introduce a texture while the film is still soft after coating. He can also limit and shape the coating on the sheet, and use different materials for coating, so attaining differing techniques both on the sheet and on the screen.

One method I have tried, as yet without success, is coating a prepared sheet with a substance like wax, drawing into the wax to expose the layer below, and then placing the sheet in a bath which contained a solvent that would dissolve the film but not the wax. This in theory is the same principle as etching. The idea is simple and it is obvious that such a technique is possible, but so far I have not had good results.

A further variant on the home-made film is a transfer paper of the Decal paper type. This consists of a heavy backing sheet with a much thinner sheet stuck to it with starch. The thinner sheet peels off easily and it is on this sheet that the various coatings can be made. Shellac can be used as well as lacquer and water-based gums, which can be screened on. They will make films that can be cut through to the backing sheet which is eventually peeled off with the help of water. But this only works with lacquer or shellac films.

REVERSAL PROCESS   This involves the use of two screens; the main advantage is that a positive mark can be achieved reasonably quickly. Besides this, two colours can be printed at almost the same time, with a degree of nuance more associated with lithography than silk-screen printing. It is akin to lithography also inasmuch as that it has to some extent the same basic principle that a surface can both accept and reject a particular substance.

Two screens of equal size are placed next to one another (Fig. 24). On screen A a stencil is made, one of several types, for example a stencil made with the blue filler previously described would be more than adequate. The image will be positive when it is realized on screen A. The ink is prepared in two consistencies: the heavier will be for screen A; the other, for screen B, will be thinner and darker. The print illustrated (Fig. 25) uses white for the first ink and a thin black ink for the second. The method is simple, though a certain degree of speed is needed. The white ink is printed on the first screen and while the print is still wet it is placed under the second screen which carries no stencil whatsoever. On this screen we have poured the thinner black ink which is printed on the still wet white print. What will happen on this second printing is that the black ink will take most readily on those parts of the paper which have no ink and not so readily, if at all, on those parts

49

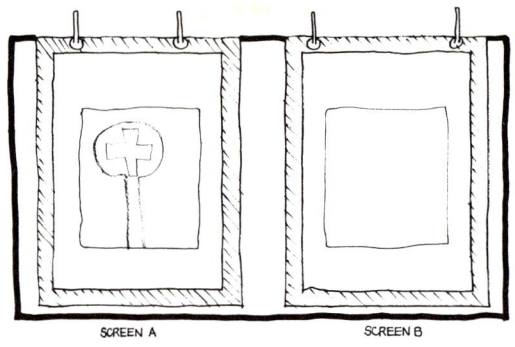

Fig. 24
Reversal process showing two screens employed

which already have one layer of wet ink. The result will be a positive print inasmuch as the marks made with the blue-filler on the first screen should be in black and the rest in white. The process depends to some extent on the different viscosities of the two inks employed. Some experimenting will probably be necessary in order to find suitable consistencies as these will depend to some extent on the conditions in which the work is carried out. If every aspect is carried out with a high degree of control then extremely subtle quality can not only be achieved but kept for large editions. If it is found that even after experimenting with various consistencies of ink the results are not as clear as required, then by stripping the final print it will be found that a greater cleanness can be achieved. This simply involves laying down on the wet print a sheet of clean paper and then this is evenly pressed by the hand all over the printed area. The paper is pulled from the print with some care to avoid smudging. In effect what this does is to take one layer of ink from the surface of the final print. Obviously any colour combination can be used to great effect and the stripping operation can also be used with a textured surface. Furthermore it is not necessary to stop at just two screens; more can be used, although the problems involved in more will demand a considerable amount of forethought on the part of the operator. Paper-cut stencils can also be used in the same manner.

OFF-SET This simply consists of printing onto an intermediary surface from which the final print is taken. The advantages of using such a technique are that a far thinner ink film is placed on the final print compared with the simple stencil methods previously described, and a variety of textures can thus be introduced. The illustration for this technique shows a paper-cut stencil printed onto a low relief collage from which the print was taken by transfer. In this way the solid areas can be broken down as well as being kept within the one print.

To do this, stick cartridge paper or some textured material onto a piece of card, making sure that there is not too much relief since this would impede printing. Put this 'plate' under a stencil-bearing screen (where printing paper is normally placed) and print. Remove it to an-

Fig. 25
Reversal process
using paper stencil

other table where it can be pressed down on the actual printing paper. Since the layer of ink will be relatively thick, hand pressure will be adequate for this operation. As long as the 'plate' is replaced in the same position under the screen each time there will be no need to clean it after each printing.

DRY PRINTING   This heading may be misleading although it is the only way to describe a process that is a natural lead-on from the last one. A 'plate' like the one described in the last paragraph is used, but for this process I would recommend a fine screen, as the image will be carried by the screen in a unique way and the finer the screen the finer the image, although if the screen is too fine it will clog with ink. Also in this process ink of thicker consistency than usual is recommended.

The procedure is as follows. The plate is placed in the printing position, under a blank screen, and a pull taken onto the plate, which is then removed and replaced by paper. The screen is then brought down onto this and pressed into contact with the paper either with a second squeegee or a roller. This effectively removes the ink left in the screen from the initial pull across the plate and transfers the resulting image onto the paper. The points to watch are not to use a plate which is in too high relief; for this would leave too heavy a deposit of ink in the screen and cause blotching or spreading of the image. Also the squeegee used should be large enough to ensure that surplus ink is well away from the final printing area.

Again it may be necessary for the operator to experiment a little with the ink consistency or with pressure on the initial pull. By replacing the plate in the same position any cleaning of the plate should be unnecessary. The ink consistency and pressure of both pulls must be consistent in order to be able to obtain an edition, but this demands no more skill than printing etchings. As the squeegee passes across the plate it is distributing not only ink but also pressure, and the pressure will vary according to what it meets in its path and leave behind an ink deposit which will be a perfect record of any pressure variation. It is this that you are relying on in this process. The print illustrated for this process consists of a collage made with cartridge paper, cotton materials and some painted marks. A cheap emulsion paint was used.

There is another similar method which will easily allow the operator to incorporate texture in a simple stencil process. It consists of taking a print, and whilst it is still wet, pressing it onto a textured surface. This is best done as a second colour overlay to allow the first colour to show through.

STENCILS THAT   One of the main disadvantages that I have found with most silk-screen
ARE STORABLE   techniques is that to store an image, the screen itself has to be stored.

Fig. 26
Dry printing process
using water-based
ink

Fig. 27
Dry printing process
using oil-based ink

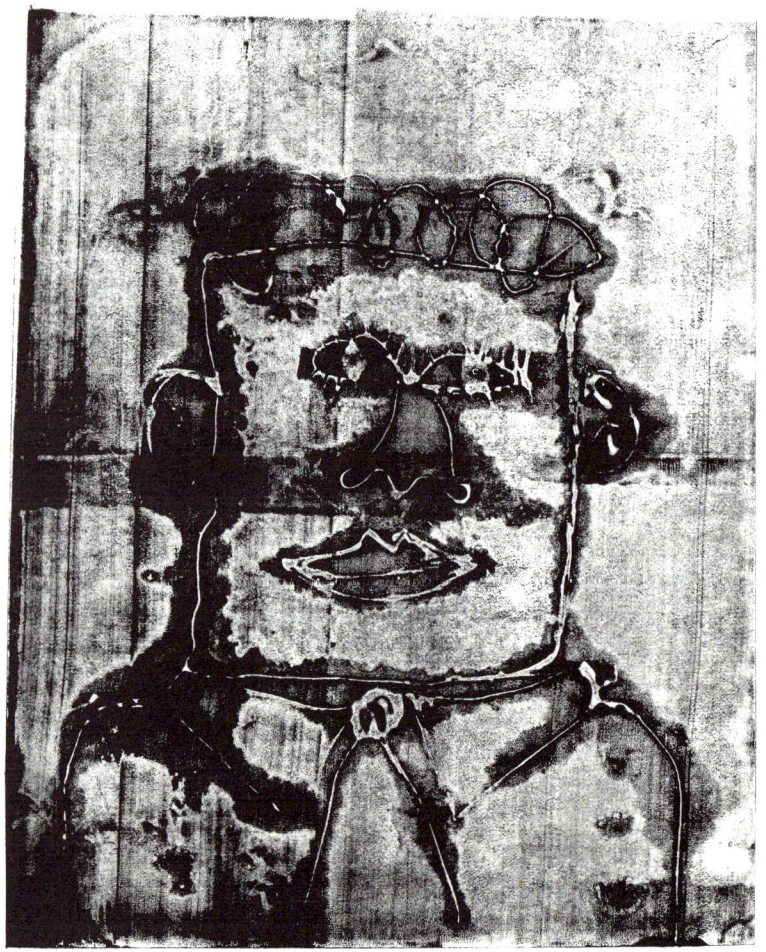

Since a screen capable of printing an imperial size image will probably cost in the region of £5 plus, the average operator can rarely afford to store images. The alternatives are that he keeps the images simple so that they can be re-cut, or that he runs the edition straight off and takes the risk of having hundreds of prints on his hands. I have tried various ways of overcoming this problem and although I must admit I have not fully succeeded, I nevertheless describe some solutions that are sufficiently developed to be worth passing on.

In theory a self-stretching frame would enable the operator to stretch silk, place an image on it, and, when the proofing is complete, take the silk off with the stencil to be re-stretched when required. There are such self-stretching frames available and they are very good. The drawback is that a piece of silk cannot be re-stretched without a certain degree of distortion; and this will certainly upset registration as well as changing the image. So the stencil must be put onto a material strong enough to carry it and allow ink to pass freely through it without any need of stretching. I use two types of material; one a plastic and the other a fine paper.

The plastic material is 'Vilene' (see p. 17). It is an open material, not like paper where the fibres are so closely matted that nothing can pass through. The Vilene fibres are criss-cross but not so close as to impede the passage of ink altogether. Stencils are attached to it in the same way as they are to silk, as an alternative to placing the stencil directly onto the screen. The disadvantages are that although the material is unaffected by oil-based inks, it expands in contact with water-based inks, and the thicker stencil deposits a thicker layer of ink on the paper. A further disadvantage is that with an image involving large areas of colour, the weight of ink within these areas has a tendency to pull the material away from the screen.

Taking a profilm stencil as an example, the procedure is quite simple. The stencil is cut in the normal way and laid down on a wad of newspaper. A piece of Vilene at least six inches larger than the image all round is cut and placed on top of the stencil with a further sheet of newspaper on top of this. Set the iron to silk heat and iron the stencil onto the Vilene, making sure in the process that all the layers are flat. You will readily see when the profilm has adhered by the amber colour on top. As with silk, make sure that the iron is not too hot and that the

Fig. 28
Cross-section of
masking used for
Vilene stencil

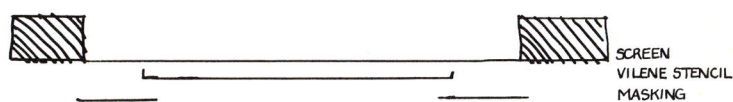
SCREEN
VILENE STENCIL
MASKING

film is not baked so that its adhesive properties are destroyed. After the ironing the backing sheet can be removed. In doing this, special care must be taken not to pull away parts of the design with the backing since some of the fibres might come away as well if the pulling is too vigorous. The stencil should now be embedded in the Vilene and be ready for printing.

A sheet of paper is placed in the printing position beneath a screen with the stencil on top of it. If there is masking to be done then this should be underneath the stencil. On the six-inch margin, double-sided adhesive tape is placed to assist in the final adhesion. The printing follows the normal procedure except that more initial pulls will be needed to get the screen well inked. Use only one pull on the final print since there is a risk of doubling up of the image by the movement of the unattached stencil. When the run is complete the stencil can be cleaned by flooding it with white spirit and gently rubbing with a rag while it is still attached to the screen. The stencil is peeled from the screen, put between two sheets of newspaper to get rid of the surplus white spirit and hung up to dry. When it is dry it can be stored indefinitely. Make sure that the stencils are stored flat and without any folds.

Most stencil techniques can be used in this manner, as long as they do not involve water-based ink. The heavier deposit of ink involved in this method is excellent for the reversal process; but it is not recommended where fine detail and delicate work is wanted since it is relatively coarse.

The paper equivalent is available in ready-prepared forms which are an adaptation of stencil paper manufactured for use with office stencil duplicating machines. There are several different makes and types. Broadly speaking only two of these are of use for screen printing.

The first is the most common. It consists of a sheet of strong open-fibre tissue paper coated with a thin layer of wax. This can be used most successfully with water-based inks, but there is a tendency for some oil-based inks to eat into the wax layer. The stencil is prepared by placing the sheet on a piece of plastic which has a distinct rough surface to allow the fully effective removal of the wax. Remember that this is a positive process and the marks made will be those that print. The image is drawn by pressing the sheet down onto the plastic with a ballpoint pen. If the sheet is held up to the light those areas that are open will be clearly seen. Certain textures can also be obtained by 'rubbing'. The completed image is placed under the screen with the edges suitably masked and the printing follows the normal procedure except that (as with the plastic material) several pulls will be necessary to get the stencil well inked. Adjustments to the image can be made by simply drawing them in after surplus ink has been removed. When the run is complete the stencil is cleaned with the appropriate solvent and stored after drying, preferably flat. Although the individual sheets are not much larger than foolscap, several sheets can be used; and, by collaging, images more associated with photographic techniques can be achieved.

The second and similar kind is based on paper coated with a fine and completely impervious plastic. This is called 'brush stencil', and allows the screen printer to achieve positive brush marks very quickly. The coating, which is yellow, is readily soluble in a liquid supplied by the manufacturers, or in ether or acetone. The sheets must be blotted several times after the liquid is brushed on to remove the dissolved plastic. When the image is complete and all the dissolved plastic blotted away, the sheet is placed under the screen and printed. Since this sheet is plastic and not wax, there is no fear of it being damaged by either oil- or water-based inks. To store this stencil, blot it with turps soaked newspaper until the ink is removed, then store it flat.

CHAPTER 6

Transfer Printing, Vacuum Forming, and Mould Blowing

TRANSFER PRINTING
This method which commercially is printing with lithographic plates or screens, is used mainly where the surface for printing on is in such relief that it cannot take a direct impression. Therefore the image is first printed onto a temporary flat surface such as transfer paper. There are two basic types of transfer paper made: simplex and duplex. Simplex paper consists of one sheet of paper coated with a water-soluble gum or albumen which acts eventually as a releasing agent. Duplex paper consists of two sheets, one a heavy backing paper to which is stuck by means of a water-soluble gum a light-weight tissue. Simplex paper is normally used for a type of transfer called 'slide on, slide off', whereas duplex is used for varnish transfer. Both of these papers can be printed with normal oil-based inks, although there are inks specially manufactured for transfer printing.

One of the major problems in printing transfers is the degree of contraction and expansion of the paper that can take place, through variations of atmospheric humidity. The difference with an imperial size sheet can be as much as a $\frac{1}{4}''$ in either direction and quite obviously this will impede accurate registration. Since the colour sequence for a duplex varnish transfer must be worked backwards (that is, the colour that will appear on top in the final image must be printed first), the problems of registration are complicated. With simplex paper the printing is the right way round and is the same as in normal printing, except that there must be a final printing of olea resin varnish (or its equivalent) to hold and strengthen the image during transfer. For both these papers any meshes can be used; but the coarser ones are best since they leave the heavier deposit of ink, which is desirable. Any type of stencil can be used.

The transferring of a simplex is fairly easy. The transfer is immersed in a tray of water for a few seconds then placed on the surface to which it is to be attached, backing side down. While it is still wet, slide the backing away with one hand, holding the design with the other. The coating that enables the design to be released from the backing now acts as an adhesive to the surface. Such a transfer can be used on a variety of surfaces such as glass, ceramics, painted wood, and hardboard.

Duplex paper for making a varnish transfer is slightly more complicated. Apart from the necessity of printing backwards after transfer, the surface to receive the image must be coated with a varnish which will act as an adhesive. When the coating has become tacky the transfer is placed in position with the printed side down, and rolled to ensure over-all contact. It is then left to dry completely, the backing paper is peeled off and the tissue is removed with a rag and water.

Duplex gives a more permanent transfer and can be readily used in the open air, whereas with the simplex this is not really possible unless finally coated with some protective varnish. The duplex can also go on a greater variety of surfaces such as unprepared wood or metal. Simplex is used on glass and to a considerable extent for ceramic printing, for which it is ideal. Ceramic inks can be printed onto simplex paper with the final varnish of a cellulose nature. Both the gum and the varnish burn away before the ink vitrifies.

Pressure transfers are probably the most recent introduction. These do not require any preparation whatsoever, they need only be pressed into place and can be made very permanent with various coatings. The basis of these transfers is the surface that takes the printed image; it is not a paper but a plastic such as polythene. This will not accept ink which is completely dry. It simply flakes off. To prevent this and also to act as a final adhesive, a pressure sensitive adhesive is screened over the whole area. (When stacked the transfer must be interleaved with a wax paper to prevent accidental sticking.) This adhesive is a stiff liquid that remains permanently tacky. When it is screened on a previously printed polythene sheet the initial layer of ink acts eventually as a releasing agent and thus only the adhesive on the back of the image transfers; the rest remains stuck to the polythene. This means that there is no surplus adhesive transferred around the image.

Printing onto canvas is being attempted more widely with varying degrees of technical success. This is not strictly speaking a textile printing problem, for the canvas is often prepared by painting on it a white ground of some sort. Most oil-based ink normally used for printing on paper becomes brittle after a period of time, having quickly lost its plasticizing agents. For other reasons normal oil inks are of little use although they have been used to a considerable extent. Transparent dyes used by textile printers cannot be treated after printing without damaging the prepared canvas and without such treatment the colours are transitory. The ideal ink for printing onto canvas is one that can hold its edge on an uneven or rough surface and will not under normal conditions lose its plasticity. Such an ink is mentioned in Chapter Three (p. 26): pigment printing ink manufactured initially for the textile industry. This is ideal for printing onto canvas as it can hold a body of colour and remain plastic indefinitely.

The canvas to be printed can be more conveniently handled if it is not on a stretcher, but if it is, a sheet of board should be inserted between canvas and stretcher as a support when printing. The canvas can be pinned to a table with thumb tacks for printing, or left loose, it depends very much on the image to be printed, the size and the number of colours, etc. If the canvas is fixed either by pinning or using a temporary adhesive, then the best method of registration is a transparent flap. This consists of a piece of transparent paper stuck down to the table along one side of the material to be printed. This should then create an overlay which covers the printing area. The screen is fixed in position, the first print taken on the overlay and allowed to dry. Subsequent prints are registered by using the overlay: the print is placed under it and all subsequent colours can be registered with it. This is only useful when doing a multi-coloured image and cannot be used when the screen is printing in more than one area.

Printing on a metallic surface is relatively straightforward. The procedure depends on the type of result required. For instance ordinary oil-based ink can be printed onto metal, but obviously it would soon come off if left outside or used in any way which would involve scratching, whereas an ink based on enamel which is baked or fired has a considerable degree of permanence. The metal is first treated so that it is absolutely clean and then a priming coat is normally applied. The cleaning process will vary with the type of metal being used. For example galvanized metal is washed in a solution of 10 oz. of copper acetate in one gallon of warm water. Aluminium alloys should be cleaned with cellulose thinners or a similar degreasing agent, not caustic solutions. The primer can be applied by brush or it can be screened on to give an even surface. The best metal primers are aluminium-based and can be bought for screen work. The ink used will determine the after treatment, if any is necessary, such as baking to achieve a greater degree of hardness.

Considering the degree of permanence and lustre obtainable, it is surprising how little screen printing onto metal has been used: it does not really need much specialized equipment unless undertaken on a large scale. Proof of the permanency of the technique can be seen in the numerous pre-war advertisements still to be found on walls around the country. The screening of enamels calls for more preparation of the metal surface to be printed. It must not only be clean but have a tooth on it in order that the ink should have a grip. The ink itself is of a highly specialized nature, being made of Frit (porcelain-enamelling base ground with water, clay, and metal oxides for colouring). The tooth is given to the surface of the metal by means of a coating, and when this is dry the enamel inks can be applied. The vitrifying of these inks restricts their use as it can only be done in a proper enamelling furnace.

Another way of printing onto metal surfaces is by the use of acid resists and subsequent etching. This was of course originally used for printed circuit work and now has been superseded by more economic methods. The use of screening to put down an image which will eventually be etched presents little or no problem as the etching can be done on a timed basis on a different day from the printing of the edition. Again I am surprised that no one appears to have used this to any extent as there are a number of possibilities in the process. The etching of plastic is quite an easy technique, the screening is made with resists which could easily be water-based gums, the plastic being 'etched' with the appropriate solvent. Printing onto glass and subsequent etching can be done in several ways. Whatever method is used, the acid for glass etching is hydrofluoric acid. This is lethal and extreme caution should be observed when using it. It can be obtained either as a powder or as a liquid. As a liquid it can be screened when mixed with a gum but this is so dangerous as to be not worth doing. The safest way of handling this acid is as a powder. The image is printed onto the glass as a gum, while the gum is still wet the acid powder is dusted onto it, the surplus being carefully removed. The powdered acid is hydroscopic and will start etching the glass straight away. When the etching is complete wash off with water. The fumes from this acid are almost as lethal as the acid itself and the operation must be carried out in a well ventilated studio and face masks should be worn. An alternative method would be to put down a screen that would resist sand blasting. Such a surface would be a screen rubber or soft plastic.

VACUUM FORMING AND PRINTING ONTO PLASTICS TO BE VACUUM FORMED

For the past few years a number of artists have used vacuum forming and blow moulding techniques, which in their industrial application have often been used in conjunction with silk-screen printing, the plastic sheet to be formed being first screen printed. It is because of this close link with silk screen and the growing interest in these particular techniques, that I have included them in this chapter. As with screen printing, the equipment and techniques described are adaptations of the commercial techniques at present employed.

In vacuum forming there are a number of different plastics used. Three of the main ones are Polystyrene, P.V.C., and acrylic. All of these are thermo-plastics as opposed to thermo-setting plastics. All of them are capable of being formed or shaped when softened by heat. The plastic comes in a variety of thicknesses and the selection of thickness depends on the final product. As a general rule the deeper the intended final image the thicker the plastic sheet must be to start with. It is possible with the above-mentioned range of plastics to get completely clear or completely white opaque plastic for printing on.

There is no particular advantage in using any particular ink. The choice will again be made according to the final result required. The ink

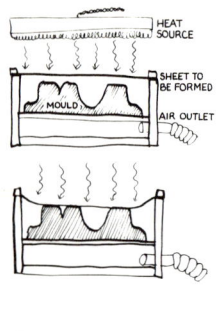

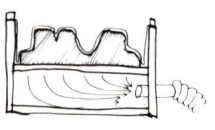

Fig. 29
Three stages in vacuum forming: sheet being heated; sheet falling on to mould; sheet being sucked down

must not affect the sheet in such a way that it softens the sheet and thus weakens it. Most normal oil-based inks will not harm the plastic although they are not designed for use in the printing of vacuum formed sheets. There are special inks designed for vacuum form work (see pp. 26–7) and the best results will be obtained with these.

Vacuum forming is very simple in theory and can be kept so in practice if the final results desired are not of an extreme nature. The theory is that a sheet of thermo-plastic is heated until softened and then sucked onto and into a mould. An instrument that I made some time ago has proved satisfactory for my purposes. I can work an image of 16" × 22" for a depth of 3". It uses a vacuum cleaner, bathroom infra-red heater, some rubber strip, and wood. The heating unit is not fixed and can be moved along the box during the operation. Some improvements can be made to this machine. One of these is the heating unit, which can be made up of a battery of circular infra-red heater bulbs so that the whole area is heated in one go evenly. There is on the market an electrical element that can be fixed in a zig-zag pattern to a sheet of asbestos and this will also give an all-over heat.

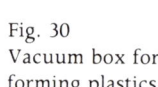

Fig. 30
Vacuum box for forming plastics

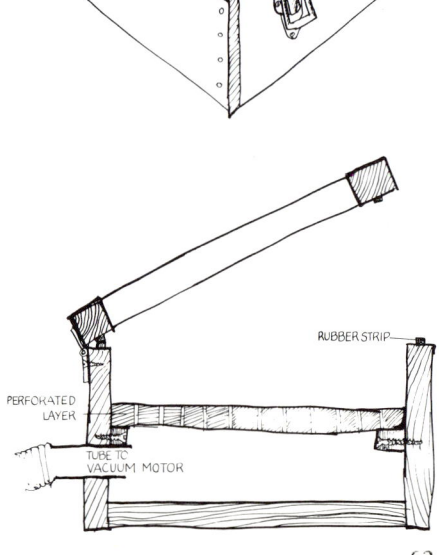

Fig. 31
Cross-section of vacuum forming box

The technique is that the mould, which can be made of any solid material (wood, plaster, etc.) is placed in the vacuum chamber, a sheet of plastic is laid over, covering the box and overlapping slightly. The clamping frame is brought into place and clamped down. The heater is then switched on and placed in position on top, resting on the clamping frame. The vacuum cleaner is also switched on and the heater moved very slowly along the box, the speed being governed by the degree of depth required. There is little or no skill in this: after a short period of trial and error it will work. The only things that can go wrong are insufficient heat getting to the plastic or insufficient force in the vacuum because of leaks in the box or a weak motor, both of which faults result in the sheet not being pulled down onto the mould adequately. But overheating of the sheet can release plasticizing agents making the sheets brittle and hard to form successfully.

In commercially made machines there are a number of developments that can be incorporated. However, the price of commercial machines is such as to put them out of reach of most artists. One major development is that when the sheet is heated sufficiently, the mould can rise up into it (this is called drape forming), and then the sheet is sucked down onto the mould. This gives the operator two advantages: a more even thickness on the final skin and the possibility of a greater depth. Another improvement is the ability to reverse the motor so that when the sheet has been formed and the heater is safely out of the way, the reversed motor helps to release the skin safely. This can be a difficult operation, particularly when the mould has some intricate parts. The versatility of vacuum forming is shown in the variety of uses to which it is put.

BLOW MOULDING   A further technique similar to that of vacuum forming is blow moulding, although in fact it is the exact opposite. A sheet is heated up and, when sufficiently soft, blown into a mould. The diagram shown is of a machine with a rather limited range of possibilities. Both vacuum

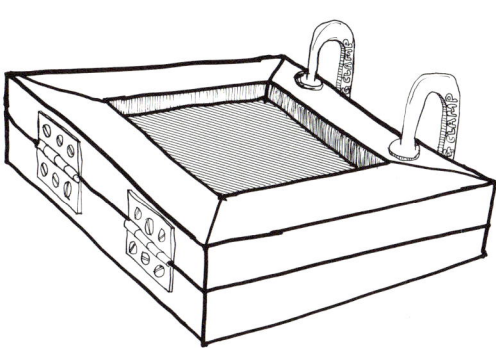

Fig. 32
Blow moulding unit

forming and blow moulding are subject to the principle, that the farther away the sheet is from the heat source the more difficult it is to maintain the correct degree of softness. In vacuum forming this is not too much of a problem, but in blow moulding, on the technical level of the machine illustrated, it is a particularly restricting problem. The heat source must be removed from the passage of the expanding plastic in order not to cause any damage to it. As this is done the sheet will immediately start to cool, so that it must be blown to the desired extent before the heat is removed. There are a number of modifications that can be made to the machine which would to some extent get around this but they would be difficult technically to achieve with the average tools available combined with average skill. Blowing should in theory be more successful than vacuum forming but the difficulties in making a machine prohibit its use. There are devices on the market which can vary the strength of the electric current to the vacuum motor. This gives a greater degree of control over both vacuum and blow moulding.

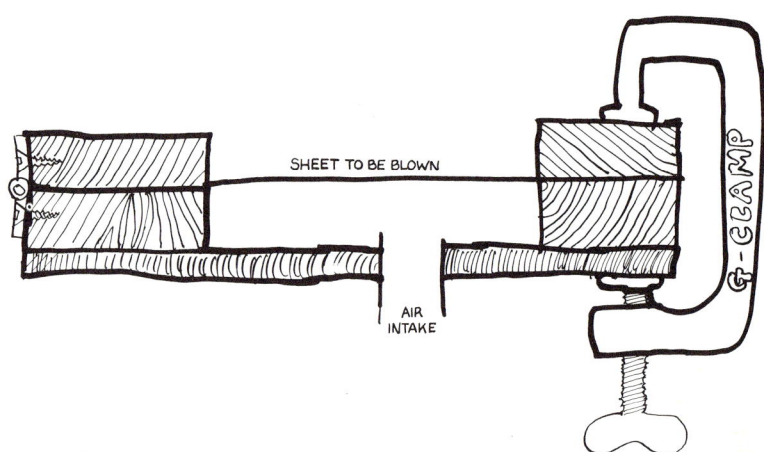

Fig. 33
Cross-section of blow moulding unit

CHAPTER 7

Photography

The history of photography goes back more than a hundred years. Throughout that time its relationship to painting has changed and changed again. Over the past decade there has been a growing interest in photography by artists, caused in part by the development of photo-mechanical printing. Often the achievement of just one or two painters is sufficient to make a particular technique acceptable both to dealers and to other painters. This is very much the case with regard to photo silk-screen printing. A good example of this could be seen in the show of Robert Rauschenberg's work at the Whitechapel Gallery in 1964 in which the canvasses incorporating photo silk-screen prints had considerable impact. Whatever the cause, the demand has been great as can be seen from the growth of photo screen printing departments in art schools up and down the country. By far the largest problems that this has brought about has been, not the understanding of the photo-mechanical technique but the finding of an image that can be transferred by this technique. It is for this reason that I have devoted this chapter to photography, hoping that it will not only help the artist to produce the images that he requires, but possibly also help to introduce him to photography in general.

Most people will not get involved with photography beyond simply taking a shot and letting someone else do the developing and printing, in the belief that it is all a bit too complicated and mysterious. This is a false premise as photography is extremely simple and the biggest drawback is that of expense. Even this can be cut down to a far smaller outlay than most people imagine. Quite obviously high quality work is more easily achieved if the standard of equipment is high, but it is not impossible to reach these standards with a minimum of equipment.

Apart from the camera, other items necessary to develop and print photographs are: an enlarger (this is not absolutely vital), developing dishes, a tank for films, and a red light for working with when printing. There are many other items, but they are not essential and it is not my intention to describe a professional set-up.

THE CAMERA Cameras can be divided into two sections for our purposes, namely plate cameras and roll film cameras. The lens is of prime importance in all cameras; it will dictate the results to a far greater extent than any other part. I shall assume, as I have done throughout this book, that the budget is low, so I shall not describe the more expensive cameras. Those I discuss all have low cost versions on the market.

The main requisite of a camera for photo-mechanical work, is that the negative size should be as large as possible, for convenience as much as for anything else. This will make far less demand on the lens when enlarging is involved. A camera that uses 35 mm. film can be used, but in order to capture enough detail the lens will have to be of a very high standard. A plate camera is ideal, for not only will it produce large negatives, but it also incorporates a ground glass viewing screen, which enables the operator to obtain the sharpest possible focus and also to estimate the general position of the image on the film area. Yet a further advantage is that a single shot can be taken and developed on its own. Although cameras using roll film are perfectly adequate, they present other problems than that of size. Reflex cameras, whilst surmounting the problems of positioning the image on the film and optimum focus, usually use 35 mm. film. Those that do not are extremely expensive, although they are available and are very good for our purposes. A twin reflex camera producing a $2\frac{1}{4}$ in. square negative is a good compromise, being available in cheaper versions. The main fault of this is parallax, i.e. the focussing lens is in a different position to that of the taking lens, and with close-up copy work from 6 ft. downwards, adjustments of a non-visual nature have to be made. The resulting image often appears half off the negative, necessitating taking the shot again, and this involves a whole new reel and not simply another plate. So a plate camera, however old it may be, is of particular value in view of the problems peculiar to photo-mechanical technique. Shutter speeds and aperture range are of less importance if, as is likely, the bulk of the work will be done in the studio. If this is the case then a good solid tripod will also be an important item.

THE ENLARGER   The enlarger will probably be the most expensive item and care should be taken in its selection. When buying an enlarger make sure that the carriage is sufficiently large to take the negatives, and that there is an arrangement that will enable you to enlarge beyond the size of the base board. This usually consists of some means of swivelling the enlarger body into a horizontal position to project the image onto a distant wall.

Apart from negative size and maximum degree of enlargement, there are other qualities to consider in an enlarger. These basically concern the light source, and the quality and type of lens, which is as important as that in the camera.

Of the three different types illustrated, the one using a cold cathode light is the best, giving a maximum of diffused light. This, however, is only available with the more expensive models used by professionals. It is more likely that a model using a condenser system will be available and it will also meet the other requirements such as negative size and maximum enlargement.

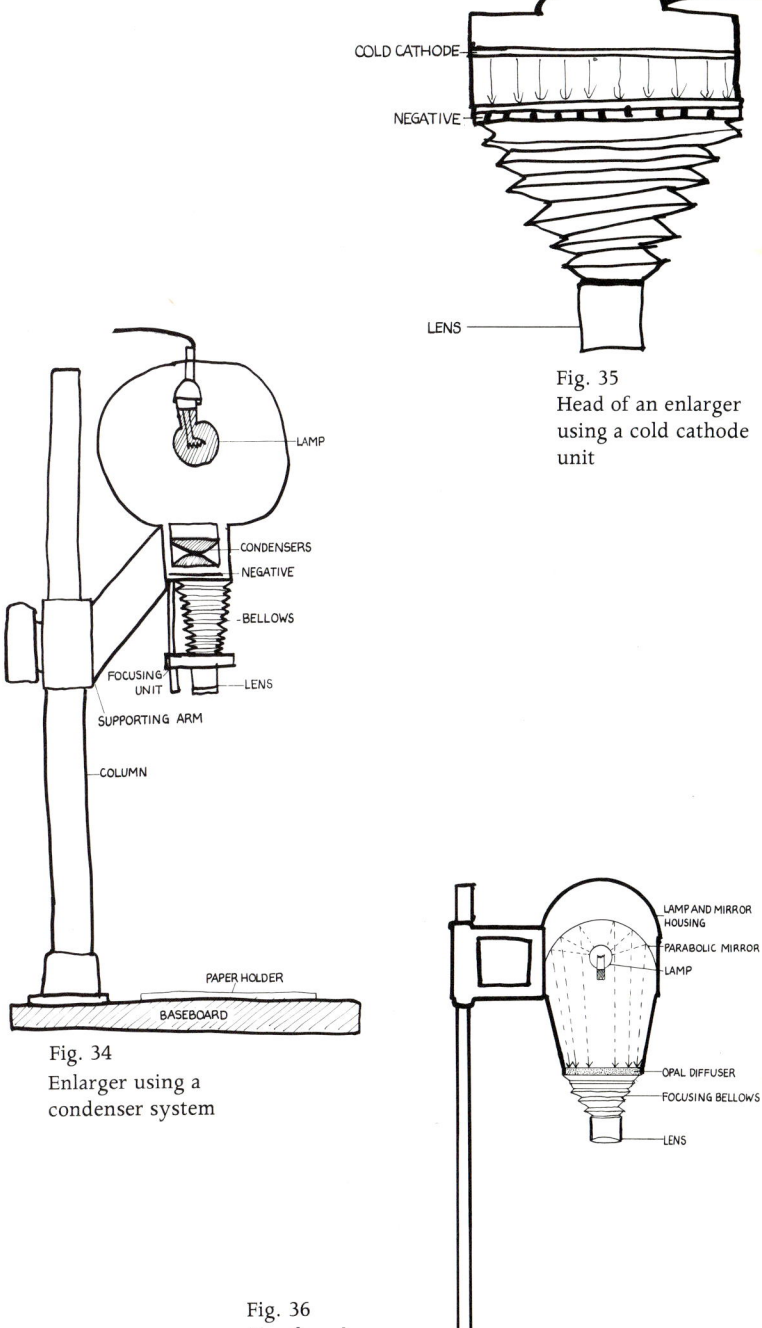

Fig. 35
Head of an enlarger using a cold cathode unit

Fig. 34
Enlarger using a condenser system

Fig. 36
Simple enlarger

67

The lens normally supplied with the enlarger will be a medium length focus lens. This will suffice for all but the most specialized jobs. A lens of shorter focal length will enable the operator to obtain a greater degree of enlargement at a shorter length. However there are certain problems involved with these lenses such as the intensity of the light dropping off towards the sides of the projected image. As problems of replacement will largely depend on the type of enlarger used, information concerning the purchase of further lenses for the enlarger should be obtained from either the dealer or manufacturer.

Almost all cameras will make an adequate substitute for an enlarger. Clamp the camera in a vertical position as if copying a book. Open up the back, place the negative where the film is normally located, position above this a light source, and make sure that there is adequate protection from heat for both the negative and the camera—and use something, such as a piece of Kodatrace to diffuse the light. Now open the shutter and focus up on the base board. It should be borne in mind that the main problem in such a set-up is that of light escaping from the light source. A makeshift way of getting over this is to drape the light source housing with some heavy material, removing it at the end of each exposure. Enlarging in this way will certainly give adequate results and may help you to make up your mind whether or not you wish to purchase an enlarger.

Another way of working without an enlarger is to use a projector replacing the slide with a negative. The major problem will be reducing the amount of light which is too much for enlarging purposes. This can be done by placing in front of the lens a piece of card that has been pierced with a pin. It may be necessary to experiment with this, varying the size of the aperture by making more than one hole in close proximity. This reduces the light and does not interfere with focussing. An alternative would be to replace the bulb with one of lower strength. This would also avoid any chance of damaging the negative with heat.

THE DEVELOPING TANK   This item of equipment is readily obtainable and although there are many different types on the market the more expensive will only be of advantage to the operator who intends to work with photography a great deal. The type I would recommend is that called Universal, which will take several different sizes of roll film. It consists of a light-proof tank in which is placed a spiral film holder. This has two plates in which there are grooves to take the film. They are placed on a tube-like axle and allow the plates to be moved up or down to accommodate the various widths of film. In order that this may be done with the accuracy necessary, a series of notches is placed on the side of the tube so that when the movable plate is pushed a spring-loaded catch will stop it at the appropriate distance. Having set the spiral at the correct spacing for the film, the next operation must be carried out in absolute darkness. It is, however, possible to buy developing tanks for daylight loading, and thus avoid the necessity of an absolutely light-proof room.

When loading the tank with film for the first time it is advisable to have everything laid out in order on a clear table top. This will help the operator to reassemble the tank in the dark correctly. The film is threaded onto the spiral in the manner recommended by the manufacturer. The backing paper, if there is any, is finally torn from the film and the threading is completed. The spiral is placed in the tank with the lid on top to seal off the light. Obviously, with the variety of tanks available, this is only a very basic guide to loading and most tanks will be supplied with adequate instructions. What is important when buying a tank is to see that it is able to do as much work as possible and is not restricted to one particular type of film. Tanks for developing plates or sheet film are fundamentally the same but without the spiral. They consist of a rectangular tank down the sides of which are grooves that take the plates or films and keep them separate. A lid covers the tank to make it light-proof and as in all tanks there is an inlet hole which allows the tank to be filled and emptied without risk of light entering. This generally serves a dual purpose, being used also for inserting a thermometer to assess the temperature of the liquid inside the tank.

It must be borne in mind that when the manufacturers of both films and tanks recommend certain conditions they are understandably describing optimum conditions for their product. These may not be absolutely necessary and may only constitute the maximum of safety. I would advise the operator to experiment and find the best conditions for himself. For example, it is recommended that panchromatic film should be developed in complete darkness; but I have found it possible to load film with some light, just enough to make it easier. If the operator finds it easier to have some light, then a simple test would be to place a piece of film in the open so that it receives the maximum amount of light that it would receive if being loaded. If this is subsequently developed and shows no signs of fogging (dark and unclear), then it would be safe to work in that amount of light. A further way to avoid the necessity for a darkroom is by using a loading bag. This simply consists of a bag made of a material such as black velvet and lined with some other dust-free material. A zip fastener allows the empty tank and film to be placed inside, and the hands can be inserted through two sleeve-like openings so that the loading operation can be carried out without any light getting in. I have loaded film into a tank successfully by getting into bed and covering myself and the tank up with the blankets. Unorthodox as this is, it works, and means that I do not have to have an area specially devoted to loading film.

There is to my knowledge no substitue for the developing tank and it is worthwhile after purchasing one to practise with it several times to minimize the risks of spoiling film.

DEVELOPING DISHES
These are used for developing photographic paper and any orthochromatic material. They are simply waterproof trays of a material, such as plastic, that will not be affected by the various chemicals used in the developing and fixing of prints. Enamelled steel is the cheapest, stainless steel the most expensive. They come in a variety of sizes and the choice should be influenced by the maximum size the operator is likely to want to work in relation to the total bulk of the work. If the operator will only occasionally want to print 20 in. $\times$ 30 in. and most of the time will print 20 in. $\times$ 16 in. or less, than it is uneconomic on the developers, etc., to have the larger dish. On those occasions when larger work is desired it is possible, if a little inconvenient, to fold the print so that it fits into the dish, making sure that it is fully immersed in the liquid. Obviously the ideal answer is to have a range of dishes that includes various sizes but the prices of dishes are extraordinarily high.

There are substitutes for manufactured dishes that are far cheaper and really just as good even if they do not necessarily look so nice. Of these the simplest is that of using an old screen. A sheet of polythene attached across the top so that when it is filled with a liquid it is supported by the screen material, is more than sufficient, particularly for the extra large work for which dishes may not be available. Another substitute is a trough used to cover strip-light fittings in the ceiling. These are generally cheaper and perfect for the job as they are made of plastic. If the operator does vacuum forming, then it is a simple matter to form a quantity of dishes. Three dishes are needed ideally for any job: (1) developing, (2) washing, and (3) fixing. The washing can be done in a sink so only two are really essential.

OTHER EQUIPMENT
A thermometer is used to assess the various temperatures of developers, etc. It is not absolutely necessary, simply reassuring. The same applies to the timer, which can play an important part when it comes to the more crucial exposures. It will not, however, automatically assure better prints. It will be found most useful in the darkroom when a sound signal is the only means of telling the time. The alarm system is also useful for long periods when one is apt to forget the time.

Drying Cabinet and Glazer. Although useful these are expensive items more necessary to the professional photographer. If they are purchased then the instructions normally supplied with them should be followed.

The operator will find that after a period of working and experimenting he will get to know and be able to judge times, temperatures, and measurements in general very accurately. Often the work he is involved in will be of an unorthodox nature where the various items used by the professional photographer would be of little use. It is assumed that in these experiments he will develop his own techniques to suit both the image he is working with and the equipment he has available. I have found that a surplus of equipment tends to inhibit because it eliminates accidental results. Perfection of technique, whilst being a very worthy objective, often ends up being rather sterile.

FILM Fundamentally there are two types of film available, orthochromatic and panchromatic. The difference between these two films is their degree and range of light-sensitiveness. Panchromatic film is sensitive to the complete colour spectrum and consequently can only be handled in darkness. Orthochromatic film and paper is insensitive to the red band and can be handled in a red or near red light. For the most part roll films tend to be panchromatic while orthochromatic film is mainly used on copy process work; the operator will have occasion to use both. The various procedures involved with the development and fixing of films and also of paper will be better understood if it is realized what the film basically consists of. A layer containing a light-sensitive substance is coated onto a plastic sheet or glass or paper. The substance mainly used is silver salts such as silver nitrate. These salts are carried in a film of gelatine or plastic with various modifications and chemical additions. Two crude but none the less workable formulae are given below. Both use silver nitrate.

(1) Paper coated with ferrous salts exposed in contact: develop in a solution of silver nitrate.

(2) Ferrous ammonium citrate and silver nitrate in C.P. gelatine coated on paper: develop with borasic or rochelle salts.

Light falling upon the film affects the silver salts according to its degree of intensity. The image is developed by causing the salts thus affected to decompose. (This process of decomposition is basically what happens when silverware stains.) The image having been developed, the surplus silver salt must be removed by immersion in a fixing solution which clears the film of surplus emulsion. This can only be done if the colloidal (gelatine) layer in the exposed areas has, in addition to turning various degrees of black, also become impervious to fixing. This is the other factor involved in the development of the image. The variety of additional chemicals that would make an orthochromatic or panchromatic film more light-sensitive (faster) or less light-sensitive (slower) are so great and complex as to be beyond the scope of a book of this nature. Suffice it to say here that there are many manuals concerning the formulae of the most specialized and of the most common films, and if the operator finds his interests in photography growing, it would be to his benefit to read to books mentioned in the bibliographies.

With all these chemicals, care should be taken when first handling them, as the operator may find he is allergic to them. A chemical that can cause irritation is ammonium bichromate. The developers for some of the orthochromatic films often contain relatively strong caustic agents which can cause some discomfort. If irritation does occur, either barrier creams or rubber gloves should be used.

Apart from manuals of a more specialized nature the operator will find useful the various catalogues that manufacturers issue with samples of papers and films. These will give him a good guide as to what is available and by consulting with the manufacturer he will be able to obtain information concerning processing of any of the products.

PHOTOGRAPHIC PAPER This is basically the same as film, the main difference being that the emulsion is coated onto paper. It is far less sensitive to light than film and is almost without exception orthochromatic and can be handled in yellow light. As with film, there is a great variety of papers available. Apart from size and weight the differences are mainly the degree of light-sensitiveness. The basic terms of describing light-sensitivity of paper is in grades of hardness, thus soft paper is more light-sensitive than hard paper and is normally used in conjunction with a negative that can be described as hard. With a soft negative, one in which there is low tonal contrast, it is advisable to use a hard paper in order to counterbalance the deficiencies. The terms soft, extra soft, medium, hard, extra hard, and so forth are universal to all manufacturers. There are various terms used to describe the same qualities, but it is enough to know the one scale. Apart from the degrees of light-sensitivity, there is a variety of weights of paper and finishes: matt, gloss, etc. These finishes have little or no effect from a strictly chemical point of view and it is for the operator to choose what he wants according to the results he wishes to obtain. It is advisable to have a selection of papers so that you are able to print most of the negatives and only have to abandon the really bad ones. I prefer to use a lightweight paper. Apart from being more economical it is easier to handle and does not curl as much as some of the heavier papers. The lighter weight paper can always be dry-mounted if necessary.

A paper worthy of special mention, as it will almost inevitably be used at one time or another, is translucent paper (T.P.). Certainly a paper very similar to this will have to be used if a transparent positive image is to be obtained economically. Translucent paper has an emulsion that gives intense blacks when developed in lith developers. This is because it has a higher concentration of silver salts. Lith developers are used in this instance to give the required density, as although the paper will develop in normal developers, the image obtained is too thin for use with photo-mechanical work. Incidentally, the finer lith material (lith is the general term for this material) such as Ortholith, make excellent black and white slides very cheaply. It is relatively simple, having developed a film, to make a contact print onto a sheet of Ortholith and develop with normal developers. Lith developer contains fairly strong caustic elements and precautions must be taken if the operator has sensitive skin.

The development of paper is fundamentally the same as developing film, the major difference being that all parts of this operation can be carried out in a safe light. Normally a yellow light will be safe, but it would be as well to check with the manufacturer's instructions supplied with the material. The exposure time for each negative will depend on the type of enlarger being used, the condition of the negative, whether it is thin or dense, and the type of paper selected. A standard check on exposure times would be to focus the image on the base board, make sure that the only light source is safe, place a sheet of unexposed paper on the base board and again make sure that a colour filter is on. Secure the paper to the board with clips or glass, take a sheet of black light-proof paper that is slightly larger than the sheet on the board, and place it so that just a strip of the unexposed sheet shows. Then expose for five seconds at the end of which the black sheet is moved to expose a further strip which in turn is exposed for a further five seconds, so that the original strip has then been exposed for ten seconds. This operation is carried on until a sufficiently broad spectrum of exposures has been made. The time interval need not be five seconds, it can be more, as long as you have at the end an image which contains some parts over-exposed and some under-exposed so that you will be able, by counting the stripes on the development, to gauge the exposure time required.

The development of the paper is divided into three stages, the middle one of which can be dispensed with. These stages are development, stopping, and fixing. Washing in water between each stage is important, with a final wash of up to half an hour in length. The test exposure is immersed in the developer which has previously been prepared according to the manufacturer's instructions. There are a variety of developers manufactured. In my opinion, the choice of what make of developer to use should be mainly based on convenience; the shelf life will be a further point to consider. The most stable forms of developer are those available in powder form as opposed to liquid. Most are available in both forms; the powder has to be made up when required, which could be inconvenient. Liquid developers need only be thinned down to the appropriate strength, but they do have a tendency to oxidize and become useless. As with most materials, substantial reductions are made by the retailer for quantity sales and it is a considerable economy to buy in bulk as long as there is no danger of the developer deteriorating over a period of time.

The same safety rules apply to the development and fixing of paper as in the case of film, and suitable precaution should be taken. The development time will vary according to the length of exposure, the type of paper used, and the developer. When the image becomes visible and when it has reached the required density it is taken from the dish, washed briefly in water and placed in a stop bath. This stops any further development of the image but is not absolutely essential, and can be replaced by a longer washing in water. The same type of fixer is used as with film, but normally weaker. After fixing, the image is washed for up to half an hour and then it is ready for drying, and glazing if required.

With the test sheet completed it will be possible to calculate fairly accurately the exposure time necessary to obtain the desired results. Obviously the more the operator works with the medium of photography the less he will need such tests. However, to start with they will be invaluable for giving examples of ranges, tonalities, etc. It is also advisable to keep the various measurements required at all stages as accurate as possible, even though eventually the operator's judgement will usually be sufficient.

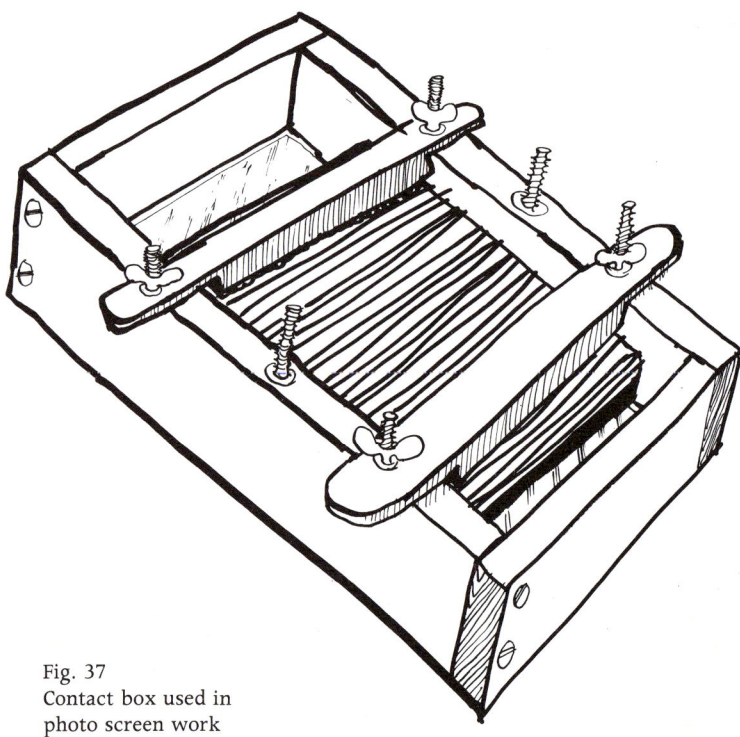

Fig. 37
Contact box used in photo screen work

CHAPTER 8

Photo Silk-screen

Photo silk-screen is in essence very simple and whatever the procedure and materials used the same basic principle applies: that light falling on a colloid containing a bichromated chemical will change the colloid and make it insoluble in a specific liquid. In order to carry out the various procedures with ease and efficiency one or two pieces of equipment are necessary.

THE CONTACT BOX   This is used to hold the transparent positives (diapositives) in intimate contact with the film being exposed. There are several different types that can be made without special skill. The one shown consists of a stout wooden frame which on the inside at one end has a lip. The inside of this lip is lined with felt and a sheet of plate glass or heavy gauge glass is placed inside. A pad slightly smaller than the inside measurement of the frame is made with a block of wood covered on one side with thick felt or a layer of foam rubber (soft plastic foam is stiff enough to make a good job). Make sure that this layer is reasonably flat if it is not covered with linen material. Projecting from two sides of the frame is a set of bolts which are aligned across the frame. Wooden bars are then made to correspond with the bolts. On the underside of each of these bars an extra piece of wood is attached so that when bolted in place it presses down the pad inside the frame. A slight improvement on this design is for the pad to be hinged down the middle and a couple of handles fixed on the back. This will make it easier to get the pad in and out without disturbing any film that might be registered up to the diapositive. A heavy sheet of glass will work as well, particularly when weights are placed on it. The contact box just makes a better job of it and eliminates to a considerable extent the possibility of an accident such as the jolting of the film during exposure.

A relatively new introduction which is another form of contact box is called a Copysac. This has been designed especially for direct sensitized work where the screen mesh itself is sensitized. It consists of a large heavy gauge polythene bag into which can be placed the material to be exposed. The bag is then sealed airtight and a tube that is connected to the bag attached to a water pump on a cold water tap; this pumps out the air and creates a vacuum which brings everything in the bag into intimate contact. This works very well not only for direct sensitized material but for indirect sensitized material as well.

LIGHT SOURCE The other major item needed is a *light source*. This must be bright enough to avoid unnecessarily long exposure. The ones most easily obtainable, as they are used by photographers, are photoflood bulbs. These come in a variety of styles, such as internally silvered which are similar to ordinary pearl bulbs, and vary in size and duration of life. All kinds get very hot compared with domestic bulbs, so shades made of material likely to melt with excessive heat should not be used. Metal shades can easily be found and are not too expensive. The best shades or reflectors are those that reflect the most light. Enamel reflectors are good; being very substantial they protect the bulb from any knocks. The number of bulbs used depends on the area being exposed and the strength of bulb.

Another light source that can be used is a mercury vapour lamp. This, like some of the photoflood bulbs, is internally silvered and thus does not need a reflector but it does need special control gear. A further light source is a carbon arc, which is probably the brightest of all; if it is available I recommend this, since it cuts exposure times considerably.

As an indication of exposure times and varying light strengths, a no. 1 photoflood at 14 in. away from the film will take approximately 20 minutes to be exposed properly. Compare that with the following and you will have some idea of the varying brilliance:

Carbon arc at 30 in.	4 minutes
Mercury vapour lamp at 20 in.	5 minutes
Direct sunlight	1/2 minutes

It must be emphasized that with all these light sources there will be variations even between the same products, and that, as in photography, it is advisable to carry out tests to assess accurately the exposure time necessary.

STENCILS There are two basic groups of photo silk-screen stencils, they go under the heading of direct and indirect. The difference between the two groups is that with indirect the whole photographic procedure is carried out on a temporary support which, when finished, is attached to the screen. In the direct stencil the screen itself is sensitized and therefore all the work is done with the screen. Over the past few years I have developed a further type of photo stencil which does not strictly speaking fall into either of these categories (see p. 82).

Direct stencils
Possibly the simplest of all the photo stencils that can be used. They consist of a colloid such as gelatine and potassium bichromate which when mixed with water gives a light-sensitive coat on drying. Apart from gelatine, which is used a lot for this purpose, it is possible to use P.V.A., and there are some manufactured liquids on the market based on P.V.A. Whichever one of these is employed it will be used as a liquid that

is coated onto the screen and allowed to dry in a darkened room. None of the direct sensitizers are panchromatic or very fast. Compared to normal photographic speed, the speeds involved in photo screen work are very slow. Not until the coating is dry does it really become light-sensitive. Light falling on the coating tans it and thus makes it insoluble in water so that when it is eventually washed in water the unexposed parts (black) are washed away, leaving the exposed parts (white), which on drying become the stencil.

Coating the screen as evenly as possible is very important, the liquid can be either brushed or flowed on. The choice depends on the size of the screen. With smaller screens it is easier to flow the liquid. However, with larger screens a soft camel-hair brush of sensible size, 2 in. upwards, is used to brush on the liquid. When flowing the liquid into a screen you will need a tray into which the surplus can drain. The screen is held in an upright position and the liquid is poured along the top side at the uppermost edge. Try to avoid it running through the mesh of the screen. When completed, the screen is taken to a darkened room. Heat can be applied to speed up the drying but too much heat will damage the coating. A second coating may be necessary if either the liquid is too thin or the mesh is a coarse one but it must only be made when the first is thoroughly dry. If a lot of direct stencils are contemplated then it will be useful to construct a box which can be heated up so that the screens can be dried quicker.

If a Copysac (see p. 75) is not being used the screens may be exposed to light by using a thin pad and a sheet of glass. The pad, which is slightly smaller than the printing areas of the screen, is laid down on a flat surface. On top of this the screen is placed with weights on the frame, so that the pad is raising the centre of the screen slightly. The diapositive is laid on top of this with the glass going on last, with some more weights to press it into better contact. It is useful to place a strip of black paper alongside the diapositive covering a part of the coated screen. This will act as an exposure guide. The exposure time will depend on two factors: (1) the strength of the light, which will be determined by the position of the light and (2) the size of the screen. The light must fall evenly all over the area to be exposed, so if the light is a single bulb and the area is large the bulb will have to be placed further away. After ten minutes has elapsed take hold of one end of the strip of black paper and carefully pull out about half an inch. This should show a distinct difference of colour between the exposed and unexposed parts. The coating, whether based on P.V.A. or gelatine, should change in colour very clearly from a pale yellow to a deep golden yellow. Keep pulling the black strip every five minutes until satisfied with the exposure. This test can be particularly useful when the diapositive being used is not of the best quality and as a result of over exposure will let light pass through the black areas. The black strip can be made to match the weakest part of the design so that the operator has some idea when those parts are beginning to be affected.

Washing or developing the screen is the next stage, and this is done with warm water. Ideally a large sink with a hot water tap and a hose is best. The screen is simply placed in the sink and warm water sprayed over it until the unexposed parts are washed away. If there is not a hot tap available then the screen can be laid on a wad of newspapers and sponged with warm water. This is a more protracted procedure but works with patience. Check that the unexposed parts are completely cleared by drying off an area and holding it up to the light. Then the whole screen must be thoroughly dried. The sides are then taped and any touching up of the stencil that might be necessary is completed.

The screen can now be printed, but on a long run it is advisable to apply a protective coating to the stencil. The selection of this protective coating is dependent on the type of ink being used. For oil-based ink use shellac or a spirit based lacquer. This is brushed across the inside of the screen. The surplus lacquer that goes onto the open areas can be rubbed away from the other side of the screen using a rag soaked in methylated spirit or a suitable lacquer solvent. Alternatively the screen can be laid on a wad of newspaper which has a sheet of some extra absorbent paper on top of it like blotting paper, so that the surplus liquid is absorbed straight through the mesh. Hold the screen up to the light to make sure that there is no coating in the open areas. If water-based inks are to be used then it is important to put the coating on both sides of the screen. Again the coating can be shellac or lacquer.

Indirect stencils
Different from direct stencils in both procedure and quality of results. The main reason for this is that with direct stencils the final image is governed by the mesh of the screen: the edge of the image must follow the mesh. The opposite is the case with indirect stencils. They are capable of holding an edge across the mesh, having been made away from the screen. It is possible to make emulsions for use as indirect stencils and it is certainly worth doing if only for economy. However, there is a variety of excellent films available on the market. These are being improved all the time and have many distinct advantages over any emulsion that is likely to be made in the studio. The manufactured films can be divided into two basic groups: those that need sensitizing and those that are already sensitized. All these films consist of an emulsion coated on a dimensionally stable plastic sheet. The two main plastics used as backing sheets are polyester and vinyl. The technique is that the emulsions are exposed and developed on the backing sheet and when completed transferred to the screen. This enables far larger photographic stencils to be handled as well as a collage of stencils in which part

of the stencil can be photographic and another part autographic. Apart from these advantages the films developed have become far finer than anything that can be hand-coated. This means that a greater degree of control can be achieved and far more delicate work contemplated. The suppliers of all the manufactured films include detailed instructions with their product, as is normal practice with photographic materials. Rather than simply repeat these instructions I will summarize the various procedures and discuss the different uses to which they can be put.

Redico/2 is a ruby coloured emulsion attached to a vinyl base by means of an adhesive which prevents it peeling off during either storage or processing. It is unsensitized and can be handled in all lights. It is sensitized by immersion or brushing with a liquid made up as follows: 6 ozs. of ammonium bichromate to 5 pints of water (60 grms. ammonium bichromate to 1 litre). This solution is called the stock and is stored away until required. It has a shelf life of approximately two months and is quite simple to make up. The sensitizing solution is then made by adding one part of stock to three parts of industrial alcohol.

A piece of film is cut slightly larger than the image to be used and a piece of brown absorbent paper is also cut slightly larger than the film. It is important that in cutting the film is not bent or kinked in any way, as this will interfere with its final adhesion to the screen. The film is placed, emulsion side uppermost, in a bath containing the sensitizing solution, and after one minute has elapsed the brown paper is placed in the bath on top of it. When a full two minutes have passed the two sheets are taken from the bath and laid together on a wad of newspaper. The surplus solution is cleaned away with absorbent material so that there is no excessive moisture on either side. The sandwich of film and paper is now light-sensitive and care should be taken in handling it at this stage.

An alternative technique can be carried out in the following way. With the film pinned to a board, brush the same solution quickly all over it with a soft wide brush, making sure that the film is covered. The brushing should take at least two minutes depending on the size of the film. If it is large, then more time should be spent brushing; the brown paper is left till last and this also is brushed thoroughly on both sides, the two sheets finally being placed together with the emulsion side in contact with the paper.

The exposure is made in a contact box with the diapositive laid on top of the vinyl backing. There is no way of telling the state of the film during the exposure as there is in the direct stencil method. Because of this it is even more important that a test exposure be carried out, especially if the quality of the diapositive is a bit dubious. A good test system is the one used in straight photography where a sheet of light-proof material is placed over the glass of the contact box and after every five minutes it is pulled off by an inch so that in the end you have the results of several different exposures on the same test and from these can select the best one. In the final exposure, strips of light-proof material placed around the outer edge of the diapositive acting as a frame will prove invaluable at a later stage.

The development of the film is carried out in warm water not exceeding 110° F. The sandwich is removed from the contact box and placed in a sink containing warm water and left for a minute or two. Pull the brown paper gently away from the film holding the film gently by the edge. Lay the film on a sheet of perspex, emulsion side uppermost, and splash or spray the warm water against it. The image should soon start to appear as a lighter red than the background. Washing should go on until the open areas are completely cleared of emulsion. A swab of cotton wool is useful particularly for the more delicate images or for the more persistent bits of emulsion—rub the surface lightly with it. Overwashing should be avoided as this will affect the adhesive qualities of the emulsion.

When the image is clear, the film is placed on a wad of newspapers and the screen, which has been thoroughly degreased with a caustic agent, is placed on top. It is helpful if the screen is wetted before it is placed on the film as this will aid any adjustment to the position of the film that may have to be made. Carefully turn the screen over with the film attached and remove all surplus moisture with absorbent material. Turn back onto a pad which is smaller than the inside measurements of the screen, placing weights on the frame so as to ensure not merely contact between mesh and film but that they are under some pressure. With a piece of cloth, press the screen into the film, taking up any surplus moisture that might be left on the top side. This then must be left until absolutely dry which may take up to twenty-four hours, de-

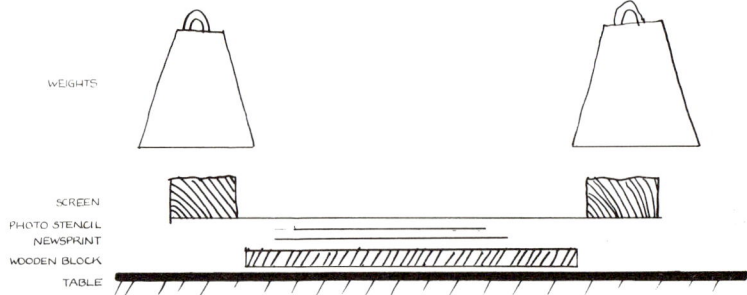

Fig. 38
Cross-section of method of attaching photostencil to the screen employing weights and block

pending on the heat in the room. It is not advisable to attempt to speed up the drying by directing a heat source at the film as this will almost certainly damage it beyond repair. It is better to have patience and wait for it to dry naturally. The backing is then peeled off; this is made easier if there is a lip free of emulsion all around (as there will be if the masking suggested earlier has been used). Peeling should be done with some care; if the image is a screen dot image then it is advisable to flood the screen with carbon tectrachloride before starting to peel off the backing. Then lightly rub the film to remove the adhesive remaining on the back. It is now ready for printing.

Redico, compared to the other films available, is substantially thicker and is a very tough film. It is capable of holding fine detail but I would recommend a thinner film for screen dot work. It will readily adhere to silk.

Plus/2 is a green emulsion on a polyester backing. It is better able to hold the fine detail of a screen dot image. It is an unsensitized film, using the same stock as Redico/2 but this is mixed with only two parts of industrial alcohol or methylated spirit instead of three. The sensitizing is the same as for Redico/2. It is considerably more light-sensitive than Redico/2 and should be handled, once sensitized, with more caution. It will adhere to nylon mesh as well as to silk. Development is the same as the previous film in all respects. The screen is degreased with a caustic solution as before and all other procedures are the same as with Redico/2. The extra speed of this film makes it useful where the diapositives being used are a bit thin. The short exposure will also be better for screen dot work as there is less chance of the dots being underbitten by the light. The final film on the screen is thinner than Redico/2 but just as durable. With both of these films all light sources can be used.

Five-star film is pre-sensitized and can be used straight from the roll without any processing. It is extremely fine film on a polyester backing. It is more light sensitive than Redico/2 but slower than Plus/2, also photoflood bulbs are unsuitable as a light source. To expose the film the uncoated side is placed in contact with the diapositive and the film is backed with a sheet of matt film. In this respect it is the same as the other films, being exposed through the backing. When the exposure is complete, before the film can be washed it must be hardened. This is done by immersing in a bath with a solution made up of one part of 20 volume strength hydrogen peroxide to 4 parts of cold water. Immersion time should be for one minute at a temperature of 65 degrees. After this, the development is the same as with the previous two films. Also the adhesion is the same. This is an ideal film for screen dot work as it is able to carry very fine detail. The removal of any of these films from the screens is done with warm water and if they prove persistent some lactic acid added to water will help the removal.

With all of these films oil-based ink only can be used. Further treatment of the stencil to make it impervious to water would be needed if water-based inks were to be used. The consistency of the ink is normally fairly thin for printing photographic stencils, particularly with screen dot work. A single pull is all that is desirable with dot work or any image containing fine detail, as a double pull or even an unnecessarily heavy pull will tend to obliterate fine detail. Once lost, it takes three pulls to regain the image cleanly. The screen must also be very tight, as any looseness will result in obliteration of the image.

There are a number of formulae for home-made films. The one I give here is typical and very useful. It is made up on a sheet of heavy manila with two coats. The first is made up of 13 ozs. of gelatine dissolved in 10 ozs. of water. This solution is flowed over the paper and allowed to set. The second coating is made up of 10 ozs. of gelatine, 1 oz. of size, and 2 ozs. of sugar. This is heated in a double boiler, and the addition of a little water will help to make it liquid. To this can be added a colouring dye such as violet. If the film is to be used within a few days then 1 oz. of potassium bichromate is added. This will mean that the film is light-sensitive once set. This second coating is flowed over the paper and allowed to set in a darkened room.

This film is exposed in a contact box with any of the normal light sources previously mentioned. After exposure, take it from the contact box and immerse in a bath of cold water for two minutes. A support that has previously been prepared is placed in a bath of hot water (100° to 110° F.) and the film, emulsion side down, is placed on top and in contact with it. The support, which can be a vinyl sheet or perspex which has been thoroughly cleaned of dust, etc., should be larger than the film. After five minutes immersion in the hot water bath the backing is peeled off carefully. The film is now attached to the support and is rocked to complete development. When the open areas are cleared of emulsion the film and support are placed in a bath of cold water. When the film is taken from the bath it is placed on a flat surface and a screen put gently on top, the surplus moisture being absorbed with blotting paper or cloth. It is then allowed to dry completely when the support is removed.

The last type of photostencil I am going to discuss is one I have developed over the past few years with considerable success. It does not strictly speaking fall into either of the previous two basic groups. A piece of Vilene or some other open matted material that can be coated is cut to the required size. This is pinned to a board and is either brush coated or flowed with any of the following solutions:

(a) 2 ozs. ammonium bichromate added to 1 pint of water—one part of this stock solution added to 5 parts P.V.A.

(b) 1 lb. of gelatine, 1 oz. potassium bichromate, 1 oz. sugar, 3 quarts boiling water.

(c) To 2 quarts boiling water add $1\frac{1}{2}$ ozs. potassium bichromate, 3 ozs. gelatine, $\frac{1}{2}$ oz. glycerine, 1 oz. borax, 1 oz. gum arabic, 12 ozs. size, $\frac{1}{2}$ oz. ammonia.

Two or three coats may be needed, allowing each coat to dry in a darkened room. When finished the sheet is treated in the same manner as the films described, and exposed in a contact box. On completion of exposure the sheet is taken from the box, immersed in warm water, and rocked to and fro. It will help if a little colouring is added to the above formulae. A violet colouring will be found suitable for this purpose. When this is complete the sheet is placed between two sheets of blotting paper and dried completely by hanging up in some warm place. The sheet is a photographic stencil and can be placed under a screen in the manner of a paper-cut stencil. If the image contains a lot of open areas then a little extra support will help. This can be a temporary adhesive such as rubber cement as long as it does not interfere with the printing areas. These stencils can be stored, if they are thoroughly cleaned, when finished with.

List of Suppliers

Process Supplies Ltd
19 Mount Pleasant
London
WC 1

They supply screen machines of all types and inks etc.

Ink Manufacturers

Coates Bros Inks Ltd
Easton Street
London
WC 1

Dane & Co Ltd
1 Sugar House Lane
London
E 15

Cellon Ltd
380 Richmond Road
Kingston
Surrey

Paper Merchants

T N Lawrence & Son
2 Bleeding Heart Yard
Greville Street
London
EC 1

Inveresk Paper Merchants Ltd
Ferry Lane Wharf
Ferry Lane
London
N 17

Photographic Suppliers

Harringay Photographic Supplies Ltd
435 Green Lanes
London
N 4

Marston & Heard
378 Lea Bridge Road
London
E 10

Index

base for screen, 12
Beggarstaff Brothers, 9
blow moulding, 63–4
blue filler, 36, 39, 42, 43, 49

Camberwell School of Art, 17
Cameras, 65–6
canvas, printing onto, 59–60
China, 7
contact box, 74–5, 79–80, 82
Copysac, 75, 77

developing dishes, 70; tanks, 68–70
development, 73–4
drape forming, 63
drying racks, 21–2

Egypt, 7
emulsion: Plus/2, 81; Redico/2, 79, 81
enlargers, 66–8
etching: comparison with 49; screening for, 60–1

film, photographic, 71
flooding, 36
frame: making of, 12–13; attachment to base, 13; self-stretching, 55

glass, liquid stencil on, 39

industrial uses, 10
ink:
 ceramic, 59
 nitro-cellulose, 24
 oil-based, 23–4, 29, 41, 43, 44, 48, 55, 56, 57, 58, 59, 60, 62, 82
 pigmented fabric, 26, 59
 plastic, 26–7
 thermographic, 27
 transfer printing, for, 58
 transparent, 23–4
 water-based, 24–5, 33, 39, 41, 43, 44, 48, 55, 56, 57
ink for printing on metal, 60
inking the screen, 30

Japan, 7
lace curtaining, 17

lithography, comparison with, 10, 42, 49
metal meshes, 17
metal, printing onto, 60–1
Nicholson, Sir William, 9
nylon, 16, 18
off-set, 50–2
organdie, 15, 18
packing-case letters, 7
paper for printing, 27–8; for stencils, 33; transfer, 58; photographic, 72
photo-screen process, 8
photo silk-screen, 65; direct, 76–8; indirect, 78–82
plastics, printing onto, 61–2
pochoir, 9
posters, 9, 10
Pryde, James, 9
pulling a print, 30–3

Rauschenberg, Robert, 65
reversal process, 49–50, 56

screen: materials for, 12–13; stretching, 18; cleaning, 18
Sharple, B., 14
silk, 15, 18
squeegees: types of, 19–20; sharpening, 19–20; using, 31–3
stencils:
 blue film, 48
 collage, 36
 french chalk, 44
 liquid, 36–41
 paper-cut, 33–6, 50
 photo, 76–83
 profilm, 47–8, 55
 wash-out, 42–4
 wax, 41–2
—storing of, 52
terylene, 17, 18
transfer printing, 58–61

U.S.A., 8

vacuum forming, 61–3
Vilene, 17, 55–6, 82

85